Entrepreneurship and Ethics in Ancient Rome

The Management Lessons of Pliny the Younger

by Robert C. Lerner

First Edition

Oshawa, Ontario

Entrepreneurship and Ethics in Ancient Rome:
The Management Lessons of Pliny The Younger
by Robert C. Lerner

Managing Editor: Kevin Aguanno
Series Editor: Mark Kozak-Holland
Typesetting: Carolyn Prior
Cover Design: Robert Lerner
eBook Conversion: Carolyn Prior

Published by:
Multi-Media Publications Inc.
1050 Simcoe St. North, Ste 110
Oshawa, ON, Canada, L1G 4W5

http://www.mmpubs.com/

All rights reserved. No part of this book may be reproduced or transmitted in any form or by any means, electronic or mechanical, including photocopying, recording or by any information storage and retrieval system, without written permission from the publisher, except for the inclusion of brief quotations in a review.

Copyright © 2013 by Multi-Media Publications Inc.

Main Cover Photo Copyright © Stephen Alvarez/National Geographic Stock

Paperback   ISBN-13: 978-1-55489-131-3
eBook Formats   ISBN-13: 978-1-55489-132-0

Published in Canada. Printed simultaneously in Canada, the United States of America, Australia and the United Kingdom.

CIP data available from the publisher.

Table of Contents

Foreword..9

Chapter 1
    Introduction.......................................13

Chapter 2
    Pliny's Epistle 8.2 27
        Lesson 1: Promote your Successes
        Lesson 2: Establish Rigorous Standards for Advisors
        Lesson 3: Align the Message with the Medium

Chapter 3
    Pliny's Business Problem..................53
        Lesson 4: Self-Deprecate in Difficult Situations

Lesson 5: Manage Crises in Person

Lesson 6: Fully Evaluate Transactional Risks

Lesson 7: Avoid Single Sourcing

Lesson 8: Encourage Competition Amongst Partners

Lesson 9: Remember Business is Personal

Chapter 4
Pliny's Constraints............85

Lesson 10: Be Fair in Business Transactions

Lesson 11: Cultivate an Ethical Business Reputation

Lesson 12: Fully Understand your Constraints

Chapter 5
Pliny's Solution...................105

Lesson 13: Ignore Complex Solutions at your own Risk

Lesson 14: Incent your Partners

Lesson 15: Micromanage your Capital

Lesson 16: Know your Audience

Lesson 17: Closely Monitor Receivables

Lesson 18: Build Long-term Buyer Relationships

Chapter 6:
Pliny's Outcome 131
Lesson 19: Delineate Investment Objectives

Lesson 20: Remain Open to New Ideas

Chapter 7
Pliny's Lessons..........................151

Appendix A
Pliny's Bio 161

Appendix B
Pliny's Comments on his Readership 179

Appendix C
Pliny's Times............................181

Appendix D
First Century Emperors 183

Appendix E
Pliny's Tuscan Vineyard.............185

Appendix F
Pliny's Will..............................187

Appendix G
Endnotes................................189

Appendix H
Bibliography..........................205

Index
Ancient Names and Places..............213

Acknowledgements

This book would have not come to fruition without the encouragement of many friends and family members. I particularly want to extend my sincere gratitude to Jerry Kappus, Shelli Mehri, Dr. Glen Wegner, Brien Naylon, Ehsan Moghimi, Julie McNamara and Judge Richard McNamara, for their early and constant support of this project. For a businessman to write of the lessons from history requires more than the confidence to do so and fortunately, I also had the invaluable support of Professor Jacqueline Carlon, whose text on Pliny inspired this book and who generously shared her knowledge of Pliny and his times. I would also like to thank Kevin Aguanno for his willingness to proceed with a business text on Pliny the Younger, Mark Kozak-Holland for his very insightful suggestions for improving the structure of this work and Chris Stanvick for her patient editing of the manuscript. Of course any errors or misinterpretation of the sources, whether ancient or modern, is solely my responsibility. Finally, I am

Entrepreneurship and Ethics in Ancient Rome

forever grateful to my wife Diane and daughters Meredith and Allie for their loving encouragement of my literary efforts.

Foreword

As Dean of The Simon School at the University of Rochester, I am particularly proud of the fact that over half of our alums a decade after their graduation are involved in some entrepreneurial venture. This is the realization of an ever-more-common ambition for MBA graduates. Starting a firm is the dream of over 70 percent of today's high school students according to a recent Gallup poll. And an overwhelming percentage of job creation is accounted for by small to mid-size startups.

Robert Lerner, the author of this book, exemplifies this entrepreneurial spirit of which our School is so proud. Bob joined the University of Rochester originally with an interest in obtaining a doctorate in astrophysics. Once on campus, however, his self-awareness led him to the realization that a Simon MBA and a career in business would be a better use of his talents and align more closely with his passions and personality.

Entrepreneurship and Ethics in Ancient Rome

Post-graduation, Bob went to work in the computer technology industry, rising through the corporate ranks at Wang Laboratories. He learned immensely from both the company's meteoric rise and subsequent fall from grace. Attaining the position of President of North American Services for the firm, Bob was responsible for half a billion dollars in business and the livelihoods of thousands of Wang employees. He realized both how much hinged on the practice of effective management and that he could make an important difference by playing a more influential leadership and entrepreneurial role. Accordingly, Bob led a management buyout of a large share of Wang's service business. With the help of a supportive board and a dedicated management team, Bob served as the CEO and President over the ensuing decade and catalyzed the company from the red to the black while growing it into a multinational computer services firm with over 3,000 employees.

Along the way, Bob sought to learn as much as he could beyond his formal training at Simon, drawing lessons from those who had mastered the practice of management and entrepreneurship. One of these teachers, Pliny, is the subject of Bob's book.

While Pliny lived nearly two millennia ago, he was an accomplished author, politician, lawyer, priest, imperial advisor, financial administrator and entrepreneur. In contrast to the commonly held but misplaced belief that today's business leaders are largely crass and not well-read, Bob's careful analysis of Pliny's correspondence uncovered some timeless insights that allowed him to become a better leader of his own computer services firm.

Foreword

This analysis is presented in this book in eminently readable form so that you too can learn how to be a better person, business leader and entrepreneur through the observations of a talented ancient Roman.

The modern-day philosopher George Santayana was fond of saying: "Those who cannot remember the past are condemned to repeat it." The converse of his observation is that those who can learn from the past will be all the better for it in terms of successfully addressing today's challenges. Thanks thus are due to Bob for what he has so judiciously assembled in this book: aptly setting the stage on which Pliny acted and then presenting not only the problems and constraints he faced but also his elegant solution and the insights to be gleaned from this solution.

The Simon School has over 12,000 alums. The diversity of their backgrounds as well as professional pursuits is striking. For example, Simon has the highest percentage of international students (over 50 percent) in its full-time graduate programs of any top tier business school and has drawn matriculants from over 130 different countries over the years and all continents, with the exception of Antarctica. Our graduates, moreover, have gone on to pursue careers that range from running Fortune 500 firms; starting entrepreneurial ventures such as MySpace, AOL International and Kronos; serving as ambassadors and prominent government officials in the United States and elsewhere in the world; and promoting the development of their local economies through positions such as the head of Citigroup in India, the vice chair of Investment Banking for the Bank of

Entrepreneurship and Ethics in Ancient Rome

China, the head of Investment Banking for Latin America for Standard Charter, the CEO of Range Rover and Mazda, NA, the head of corporate strategy for ING and the CEO of Trimble Navigation. We are immensely proud and grateful to count Robert Lerner as an alum of the Simon School. You will find out why through reading his scholarship on Pliny and learning how it benefited his own modern-day practice of leadership and entrepreneurship — as it can similarly benefit yours.

— Mark Zupan, Dean and Professor of
Economics and Public Policy,
Simon School, University of Rochester

CHAPTER **1**

Introduction

A wealthy resident of Rome returning from his country estate in Tuscany commented to a friend:

"Other people visit their estates to come away richer than before but I go only to return the poorer."[1]

Lighthearted banter in a note to a friend regarding the shortcomings of a business venture is certainly not uncommon for any businessperson. However, this was no common businessman, for this gentleman farmer wrote of a visit to his Tuscan vineyards over 1900 years ago, in the fall[2] of 107 AD following a problematic harvest.[3] The disappointed businessman and letter writer was Gaius Plinius

Entrepreneurship and Ethics in Ancient Rome

Caecilius Secundus; better known today as Pliny the Younger (in this text he will simply be referred to as Pliny).

Pliny communicated his financial lament to a friend and business associate, Calvisius Rufus, in a letter in which Pliny also took the time to describe in great detail both the issues associated with his sale of the season's grape harvest and the actions he took in response to those issues. In so doing, Pliny created a very effective model for managing his business interests and obviously did so without the benefit of the information and communication technologies that we have become so dependent upon in our daily business lives today. However, the absence of modern management tools only serves to highlight the importance of Pliny's approach to problem analysis and business management; from Pliny's correspondence to his ancient associate, lessons can be extracted that are directly applicable to many of the business issues faced by today's entrepreneurs.

Pliny did not just write this one letter that was fortuitously preserved for posterity but rather over the course of many years he compiled and published 247 letters in nine books that survived nearly intact and are available for today's readers. Additionally another set of more than 100 letters from Pliny to the Emperor Trajan, along with many of Trajan's responses, also survived and is accessible to us as well. One must assume that, for any of the letters to have survived at all, let alone in such quantity, Pliny's books (and speeches) were very widely read among the elite (see Appendix B for Pliny's comments on his readership).

1 - Introduction

Pliny was however, more than an author; he was also a Roman Senator, imperial advisor, lawyer, priest, financial administrator and an entrepreneurial businessman. As such, Pliny frequently corresponded not just with the Emperor Trajan but also the historian Tacitus (author of the *Annals and Histories*), the imperial biographer Suetonius (author of *The Twelve Caesars*) and over 125 other lesser known men and women on topics ranging from law, oratory, politics, government administration, art, literature, history and domestic matters which included his personal business interests.

Two of the three most famous letters[4] for which Pliny is best known were addressed to Tacitus and detailed Pliny's personal experience with the eruption of Mt. Vesuvius in August 79 AD (which, along with the destruction of Pompeii, resulted in the death of his uncle, Pliny the Elder, who was attempting to rescue victims of that horrific natural disaster). Although the two letters to Tacitus were written nearly two decades after the cataclysm, the account of what Pliny witnessed as a 17-year-old youth was so precise that today the type of volcanic eruption described in his letters is known as a Plinian Eruption. The letters also enabled Pliny's birth to be dated to approximately 61 or 62 AD based upon Pliny's acknowledgement of his age at the time of the eruption.

The third letter[5] of particular note was written by Pliny to the Emperor Trajan while Pliny was serving as a special imperial envoy to a remote province and dealt with Pliny's growing problem with an approach to handling what he called a

Entrepreneurship and Ethics in Ancient Rome

"degenerate sort of cult"[6] of early Christians. This letter of Pliny's was written less than a century after the crucifixion of Jesus and no more than half a century after the execution of St. Peter and St. Paul.

Clearly Pliny was a witness to and participant in events that still resonate today. His unique position in society combined with the survival of his letters make him an especially fascinating figure for both historians and economists. For example, Richard Duncan-Jones, in *The Economy of the Roman Empire*, begins his study with an examination of a wealthy Roman Senator's finances – Pliny's, for Pliny's letters offer the most comprehensive (but far from complete) set of data pertaining to any ancient Roman Senator. However, when I first read Pliny's letters in the late 1970s as a newly-minted MBA just starting out in my career, so much of their content appeared to me as superficial and pedantic that it was easy for me to dismiss Pliny as a somewhat stuffy bureaucrat in ancient Rome with limited relevance to my entrepreneurial aspirations, or so I thought at the time.

Ignoring Pliny in my youth was far from my only mistake but fortunately was one that could be rectified, albeit more than thirty years later. During the intervening years, without the benefit of Pliny's advice and counsel, I pursued a career in the computer technology industry with Wang Laboratories,[7] and enjoyed wild company growth in the early 1980s. I then survived the many rounds of layoffs that followed that unbridled success, which ended with a highly publicized corporate bankruptcy in 1992. Wang managed to successfully emerge from bankruptcy in 1993 (as Wang Global) only to endure

1 - Introduction

years of industry consolidation both as an acquirer and finally as an acquiree. During this tumultuous time I rose to President of the North American Services business, responsible for thousands of employees and more than half a billion dollars of business.

Following Wang Global's acquisition by a European company in 1999, I had had enough of the business leadership of others and was fortunate enough to be positioned to lead a management buyout of a major portion of the U.S. service division that I had been managing. Over the following decade, my management team and I, with a supportive board, engineered our company's growth into a multinational computer services firm with a workforce of over three thousand dedicated employees. As the company's President and CEO, I never stopped learning and never stopped listening but eventually stopped loving what I was doing and at that point stepped down from all my responsibilities at the company and retired in 2009.

In the year leading up to my self-imposed departure from the daily struggles of the business world, I fortunately revisited Pliny's letters and found that my approach to business management, which evolved over many challenging years, surprisingly reflected much of Pliny's philosophy of managing his interests. Experience had taught me how relevant Pliny's counsel could be to modern entrepreneurs and business managers alike (as well as the naivete of some the opinions I held in my youth). I may have missed the opportunity to learn from Pliny early in my career but now clearly recognize the benefits of the ancient wisdom

Entrepreneurship and Ethics in Ancient Rome

contained within Pliny's missives. Additionally, despite a sea of modern business books available in the marketplace, it seemed to me that lessons drawn from Pliny's ancient business experiences, entrepreneurial outlook and ethical behavior would be of great interest to modern readers interested in the essentials of business management.

The luxury of retirement afforded me the leisure to delve much deeper into Pliny's literary work and along the way I also found that I was far from alone in recognizing the importance of Pliny's counsel. Over the last couple of decades, scholars have rediscovered Pliny and have done so with far more intelligence and eloquence than I can ever hope to bring to the subject; however, I also felt that there was a need to study Pliny the businessman and to do so from the perspective of a business executive. For I believe, unless you have been well tested by the day-to-day stresses of the business world, you cannot fully recognize and appreciate Pliny's entrepreneurial insights, depth of analysis or the wisdom of his business decisions.

Although the seminal commentary on Pliny's letters remains *The Letters of Pliny* by A. N. Sherwin-White, written in 1966, I was especially captivated, so to speak, by *Pliny's Women*. Written by Professor Jacqueline M. Carlon and published in 2009, the text convinced me that Pliny was far more multidimensional than I first understood and hence encouraged me in my efforts to study in detail his responses to the business issues he faced. The text further encouraged me to attempt to bridge the nearly two millennia separating Pliny from the modern entrepreneur.

1 - Introduction

The final impetus for writing this book was an absolute fascination with one letter of Pliny's in particular. Pliny's Letter 2 in Book 8 (also referred to as Epistle 8.2), from which this text's initial quote was taken, dealt with the management of his Tuscan estate, included a situational analysis of a business problem faced – a problematic grape harvest - and also detailed the innovative solution that Pliny implemented to assist his financially distressed grape buyers. A genuine concern of Pliny's for his buyers struck me as radical in his day and even more so in the present day in which major corporations frequently offshore operations as a strategic means to cut costs often without sufficient regard to the devastating impact such a move has on a company's domestic employees and partners. We will see that the program Pliny implemented for his partners in 107 AD was progressive and admirable in his day and remains so in ours, nearly 20 centuries later.

It is, however, very important to note, as Professor Carlon warns us early in her text: "Even the most casual of written communication is fashioned to some extent by its author for the eye of the reader..."[8] So although I used the phrase "genuine concern for buyers" above, we must be cautious and always remember that Pliny was writing letters that were most likely edited for publication and, despite Pliny's claim in the first letter of his book that: "I have now made a collection (of letters) ... (I) am taking them as they came to my hand,"[9] Pliny most likely was not. In his 1999 study, *The Anxieties of Pliny the Younger*, Stanley Hoffer noted that Pliny "presents his letters as an authentic record of an ideal person at an ideal time in which neither agonizing decisions nor regrets ever arise."[10]

Though Pliny's letters may have been subject to some editing by him to omit much of the tumult and uncertainty of daily life, with respect to Letter 8.2, we have a piece of correspondence that remained dedicated to the resolution of a business problem faced by an ancient landowner – the effects of a problematic grape harvest on both the seller (Pliny) and the buyers of his grapes (partners). Pliny's analysis of the problem and his development of a fair solution is detailed in his letter to Calvisius Rufus but is at times frustratingly vague. We must, therefore, on occasion make inferences as to Pliny's rationale underlying his actions but we never lose the fundamental elements that form the foundation of Pliny's entrepreneurial and ethical approach to business management. Based on Pliny's business management techniques and, despite our occasional contextual limitations, we are able to formulate 20 specific lessons applicable to today's business environment. These management lessons discuss topics such as personal leadership, business ethics, risk management, financial management and innovation. My hope is that through these lessons, complemented with a bit of both ancient and contemporary wisdom, a new generation of entrepreneurs and business managers will be better prepared for the challenges they will face in the unforgiving global marketplace of the modern world.

Before we begin looking at Pliny's Epistle 8.2 and its associated business lessons, let us first take a look, as one would with any modern day business consultant, at Pliny's qualifications to be our mentor

1 - Introduction

and guide. It turns out that we do have a significant amount of information from the historical record (much of it left by Pliny himself) to detail those qualifications. In fact, we have sufficient detail on Pliny's professional and personal life as well as a timeline of major career assignments in Pliny's lifetime to allow the construction of a facsimile of a modern résumé for Pliny. Pliny's "résumé" concludes this introductory chapter.

Readers interested in a much more detailed examination of Pliny's career as well as the external pressures that influenced Pliny's actions should continue on to Appendix A, entitled "Pliny's Bio" (also see Appendix C for a brief description of late first century Rome and Appendix D for a list of first century Roman Emperors).

> Author's note with regard to the ancient unit of money used within the text:
>
> Although ancient to modern comparisons are problematic, one sesterce (also shown as HS 1) was valued at 1/100th of a gold aureus and based upon today's price of gold may be converted to approximately $4.00 today. A different gold valuation or commodity comparison (e.g. silver, wheat, etc.) would yield a very different value relationship.

Entrepreneurship and Ethics in Ancient Rome

Pliny's Résumé

Gaius Plinius Caecilius Secundus　　　　　　　　　Rome

Imperial Envoy to Bithynia-Pontus　　　110-112/3 AD
Appointed Imperial Envoy to govern the province of Bithynia-Pontus in Asia Minor (part of modern day Turkey) by the Emperor Trajan. Audited provincial expenditures and found fiscal malfeasance as well as the mismanagement of building projects. Restructured provincial finances and re-initiated provincial construction projects. Investigated Christians in the province and in consultation with the Emperor Trajan, implemented the Emperor's directive of not actively seeking out members of the cult. (Note: Pliny, born in 61 or 62 AD, died while still serving in office in 112/3 AD.)

Overseer of Tiber River Conservancy Board 104-106 AD
Responsibilities for this three-year assignment overseeing the Tiber River Conservancy Board for the Emperor Trajan included both keeping the Tiber's riverbanks in repair to reduce the risk of Rome flooding and supervising the maintenance of Rome's sewage systems. (Note: Pliny additionally served as an advisor to the Emperor during this period.)

Augur　　　　　　　　　　　　　　　　　　103 AD
Installed as Augur by the Emperor Trajan. This lifetime appointment to a senior post in the Roman priesthood was achieved even earlier than that of the great Cicero. Responsibilities included taking the auspices to divine the will of the gods. (Note: This ancient ceremony performed prior to a major undertaking often involved the study of the sky for lightning and the flight patterns of birds to determine whether the gods were in favor of the undertaking.)

1 - Introduction

Roman Consul   **100 AD**
Elevated to the office of Consul of Rome by the Emperor Trajan, who was Nerva's adopted son and successor. As consul, delivered on behalf of the Roman Senate a panegyric to the Emperor. (Note: For centuries this office was the most powerful administrative position in the Roman Republic and was held by such legendary Romans as Julius Caesar, Pompey the Great and Cicero. However, under the Emperors the office was reduced to a ceremonial post. In fact, the Emperor Caligula who ruled Rome from 37 to 41 AD threatened to make his horse a consul. Despite this, the position of consul still remained the highest political honor a man could achieve.)

Prefect of the Treasury of Saturn   **98-100 AD**
Following Domitian's assassination appointed by the deified Emperor Nerva as prefect for the state treasury which was located in the temple of Saturn. This senior financial position included significant and broad responsibilities for the management of state finances.

Prefect for Military Finances   **94-96 AD**
Named prefect for military finances by the Emperor Domitian. Responsibilities included dispersing military pensions from taxes collected on inheritances and sales at auction.

Senator   **(Beginning in) 87 AD**
Enrolled in the Senate of Rome by the Emperor Domitian.[11] Served in positions that included responsibilities in the areas of state taxes and finances (Quaestor in 87 AD), civil administration (Plebian Tribune in 91) and the judiciary (Praetor in 93 AD). (Note: There is much scholarly debate around Pliny's Tribunate and Praetorship dates. Earlier dates would be indicative of Pliny being favored by the tyrannical Emperor Domitian while a later date would be more demonstrative of Pliny's distance from the "bad" Domitian.)

Entrepreneurship and Ethics in Ancient Rome

Military Tribune   2/83 AD
Served as a staff officer for the 3rd Gallic Legion stationed in Syria. Conducted audits of the accounts for the cavalry and infantry divisions finding examples of both dishonesty and carelessness.

Advocate   80/81 AD
Began arguing cases involving property rights such as wills and inheritance in the Centumviral (Civil) Court in Rome in 80/81 AD. Served as presiding judge for the court on a rotational basis. (Note: Pliny continued to argue cases throughout his career as time and responsibilities allowed.)

Education
Educated in Rome by the eminent Quintilian at his much respected school of rhetoric.

Personal
Married (no children)

Interested in: literature, writing, viticulture and philanthropy. Philanthropic activities include the construction of public baths, providing educational support of the children of Comum and funding an annual dinner for the citizenry of Comum. (Note: Pliny's hometown was the ancient city of Comum, now Como. The majority of Pliny's income was produced from his multiple estates in and around Comum and Tuscany. That income is estimated to have exceeded $4M annually.)

1 - Introduction

Figure 1.1: Shows an aureus depicting the despotic Emperor Domitian, the first emperor served by Pliny[12]. (Courtesy of Classical Numismatic Group, Inc. http://www.cngcoins.com)

Figure 1.2: Shows an aureus depicting the Emperor Nerva. Nerva succeeded the Emperor Domitian upon his assassination.[13] (Courtesy of Classical Numismatic Group, Inc. http://www.cngcoins.com)

Figure 1.3: Aureus depicting the Emperor Trajan under whom Pliny rose to the apex of his career.[14] (Courtesy of Classical Numismatic Group, Inc. http://www.cngcoins.com)

Figure 1.4: Illustration of a Roman Augur holding his religious staff. The Emperor Trajan appointed Pliny to this senior Roman religious position in 103 AD.[15]

CHAPTER 2

Pliny's Epistle 8.2

Now on to the business paradigm crafted by Pliny. Our study of Plinian entrepreneurship will focus extensively on his Epistle 8.2, which is composed of just fifteen sentences when translated from Latin into English. Nevertheless, the letter evinces a powerful and innovative business archetype that still functions effectively today. Pliny's methodological approach to managing his Tuscan estate's vineyard (see Appendix E for Pliny's description of his vineyard) will be further reinforced with specific examples drawn from additional Pliny letters as well as other ancient sources, many contemporary to Pliny's era.

Background on the Ancient Wine Business

A brief comment on the subject matter of Epistle 8.2 is needed before we begin with our analysis. We will see below that Pliny was a serious landowner who repeatedly in his letters wrote of harvest problems from which he supposedly suffered. However, the content of Epistle 8.2, as mentioned earlier, is somewhat unique in that Pliny was focused on a business problem that involved not just his properties and him but also grape buyers and a weak market for his grape harvest. It should come as no surprise that the ancient Roman elite, for whom the most respected and honorable means of making money was agriculture, were consumed with various aspects of the wine trade -- especially the profitable business of grape growing.

The Business of Wine was of Interest to the Emperors

Issues affecting grape growing therefore did not stop at the edge of a vineyard and in fact they could reach as high as the emperor himself. For example, Suetonius wrote of the Emperor Domitian:

> "Once, upon the occasion of a plentiful wine crop, attended with a scarcity of grain, thinking that the fields were neglected through too much attention to the vineyards, he made an edict forbidding anyone to plant more vines in Italy and ordering that the vineyards in the provinces be cut down, or but half of them at most be left standing; but he did not persist in carrying out the measure."[16]

Grape growing was clearly important to the Roman state, as was the pricing of the resulting product – wine. This is seen in a second example, also from Suetonius, detailing the reaction of the Emperor Augustus to complaints about wine prices:

> " When the people complained of the scarcity and high price of wine, he (Augustus) sharply rebuked them by saying: My son-in-law Agrippa has taken good care, by building several aqueducts, that men shall not go thirsty."[17]

2 - Pliny's Epistle 8.2

Both of these examples show that issues affecting the wine business were significant enough to draw the attention and the occasional ire of the emperors.

Figure 2.1: Shows a marble statue of the Emperor Augustus. Augustus, who when frustrated by complaints about the high price of wine, reminded the people of Rome that they could always drink water to slake their thirst.[18]

Pliny the Elder Wrote Extensively on Viticulture

It is therefore not surprising that wine would be the subject of the ancient poets, playwrights and of course the Plinys.

Pliny's uncle, Pliny the Elder, devoted not just a letter or two to the subject but dedicated an entire book (of his 37 books of *Natural History*) to grape growing and wine. The Elder Pliny also felt the subject was sufficiently important to even document examples of what wine was served, by whom and when, such as: "(Julius) Caesar at a banquet during his third consulship provided Falernian, Chian, Lesbian and Mamertine: this is known to be the first occasion on which four kinds of wine were served."[19] These wines served by Caesar originated in Italy, the Greek Isle of Chios, the Greek Isle of Lesbos and Sicily, respectively, demonstrating that the production and transport of wine truly spanned the empire.

Pliny's Complete Epistle 8.2

We have established that wine was a very serious business and can safely assume that Pliny was far from alone in attempting to deal with the vagaries of a grape harvest and its associated markets; so now let us move on to Epistle 8.2 which is first presented here in its entirety. We will then proceed to break the missive down into smaller components that can be examined and better mapped into today's business environment.

Below is Pliny's letter from the fall of 107 AD, written to Calvisius Rufus and translated from the Latin by Betty Radice:[20]

> "Other people visit their estates to come away richer than before but I go only to return the poorer. I had sold my grape harvest to the dealers who were eager to buy, when the price quoted at the time was tempting and prospects seemed good. Their hopes were frustrated.
>
> It should have been simple to give them all the same rebate but hardly fair and I hold the view that one of

2 - Pliny's Epistle 8.2

the most important things in life is to practice justice in private as in public life, in small matters as in great and apply it to one's own affairs no less than to other people's. For if we say with the Stoics that 'all offences are equal' the same applies to merits.

Accordingly I returned to everyone an eighth of the sum he had spent so that 'none should depart without a gift of mine.' Then I made a special provision for those who had invested very large sums in their purchase, since they had been of greater service to me and theirs was the greater loss.

I therefore allowed everyone whose purchases had cost him more than 10,000 sesterces a tenth of anything he had spent above the 10,000, in addition to the original eighth which was sort of a special grant. I am afraid I have put it badly; let me try to make my calculations clearer. Suppose someone had offered the sum of 15,000 sesterces; he would receive an eighth of 15,000 plus a tenth of 5,000.

Moreover, in view of the fact that some people had paid down large installments of what they owed, while others had paid little or nothing, I thought it most unfair to treat them all with the same generosity in granting a rebate when they had not been equally conscientious in discharging their debts. Once more, I therefore allowed another tenth of the sum received to those who paid. This seemed a suitable way both of expressing my gratitude to each individual according to his past merits and of encouraging them all not only to buy from me in the future but also to pay their debts.

> *My system – or my good nature – has cost me a lot but it has been worth it. The whole district is praising the novelty of my rebate and the way in which it was carried out and the people I classified and graded instead of measuring all with the same rod, so to speak, have departed feeling obliged to me in proportion to their honest worth and satisfied that I am not a person who 'holds in equal honor the wicked and the good.'"*

Pliny's Motivation for Writing his Letter

Given the importance of agriculture to the elite in ancient Rome and the fact that Pliny's Tuscan estate produced nearly 40% of his estimated annual income, we can assume that grapes comprised a significant portion of the Tuscan estate's cash crop and therefore viticulture would have been extremely important to Pliny. That importance alone, however, does not explain Pliny's motivation in writing this letter but we can surmise that the perception of Pliny in his home district where Calvisius Rufus resided (as well as across the upper social strata of the empire with the letter's later inclusion in Pliny's book) would potentially be enhanced with the sharing of this letter's content. Anyone in Pliny's wide circle of friends who owned farming estates should have had an interest in a successful program that might benefit their operations in the future.

Additionally, if Pliny's peers learned how Pliny proactively reacted to the challenging circumstances he faced, they would perhaps be impressed by both his generosity (as demonstrated in the letter) as well as his intelligent and creative response to the problems engendered by a difficult harvest season.

2 - *Pliny's Epistle 8.2*

The result then of writing this letter was a win-win for Pliny – tactically Pliny successfully navigated a local farm crisis and strategically Pliny further buffed his image with Rome's elite via the additional esteem obtained from the wide sharing of his successful program.

Recognizing the benefits that accrued to Pliny by the writing of this letter still does not completely address the issue of Pliny's motivation. We must also try to determine which came first, the need for an attentive businessman to address the issues resulting from a problematic harvest or an attention-seeking opportunist acting out of pure self-interest. Let us first look at Pliny's other correspondence for an insight into his actions. Despite what we discussed earlier regarding Pliny's craving for fame, we can see in one of the earliest of his letters that Pliny makes the point of proclaiming "Fame should be the result, not the purpose of our conduct..."[21] Pliny went on to say in that same letter: "But when people accompany their generous deeds with words, they are thought not to be proud of having performed them but to be performing them in order to have something to be proud of."[22]

Based on these statements, we can safely assume that Pliny was aware that there was a risk in the wide dissemination of his program if his actions were deemed foolish or inappropriate. If so, he may very well have been accused of undue self-aggrandizement – but he accepted that risk and wrote Letter 8.2. We must also remember that in ancient Rome, unlike today, modesty was not a virtue and meaningful achievements were to be promoted.

Entrepreneurship and Ethics in Ancient Rome

We should therefore note that Letter 8.2's careful construction and eventual publication could be viewed as a microcosm of Pliny's efforts to leverage his actions into recognition and fame. Professor Henderson, commenting on Pliny's literary work, writes in his book *Pliny's Statue*: "Thus, while Pliny's epistles variously picture Rome, Roman writers and Roman lives, they all portray their artist, at work in his chosen medium of words."[23] Henderson makes an even stronger claim in his book's preface when he calls Pliny's compendium of letters "a monument to self-mythologization."[24] So, we must acknowledge that despite his occasional protests to the contrary, Pliny at times strays from his principle of purity of action to that of an unabashed pursuer of reputation.

Further Comments on Pliny's Motives

With respect to Pliny's motivation in creating Letter 8.2, we cannot be completely assured that in this instance Pliny was acting in line with his stated principle of allowing fame to result from his good conduct and not vice versa. We can, however, speculate as to Pliny's order of action if we begin by first granting Pliny the benefit of the doubt and accept that he was, in fact, genuinely well-intentioned in his initial actions intended to mitigate the financial damage to his buyers (and perhaps avoid long-term damage to his estate's business). If we begin with that premise, a potential chronology for Epistle 8.2's construction and dissemination (assuming the letter was actually sent to Calvisius Rufus) is a follows:

2 - Pliny's Epistle 8.2

Potential Chronology

1. Pliny ensured he was onsite during the harvest.
2. Pliny listened to the buyers' frustration.
3. Pliny understood the need for buyer compensation.
4. Pliny conceived of a rebate as a solution.
5. Pliny designed the rebate program.
6. Pliny communicated the rebate structure to the buyers.
7. Pliny's program was met with buyer approval.
8. Pliny's program was applauded by his neighbors.
9. Pliny returned to Rome.
10. Pliny wrote to Calvisius Rufus of the program.
11. Pliny decided to include this letter in Book 8.
12. Pliny edited the letter prior to publication.

This chronology indicates that the construction and rollout of such a complex rebate scheme to multiple grape buyers would have required extensive effort on Pliny's behalf and casts doubt on the idea that the program would have been created by Pliny merely for public consumption and image making. In fact, any chronology documenting such a complex effort would likely support our initial assumption that good conduct in this instance preceded

Entrepreneurship and Ethics in Ancient Rome

self-promotion. That said, we must still allow for the possibility that, following the initial recognition for and conception of the rebate program's need (steps 3 and 4 above), Pliny allowed the idea of future publication to infiltrate his thought process for the program's design (as early as step 5) and enhanced it accordingly. We should never doubt that self-promotion was at any time far from Pliny's thoughts.

Interestingly, in this letter, Pliny also dwelled extensively on the mechanics of the rebate and also included an example calculation of a rebate. These details could have been easily dropped at the time of publication (as it appears he dropped dimensions from other correspondence dealing with construction issues) but their inclusion reinforces the interpretation that Pliny sought to ensure that he thoroughly instructed his readers in the particulars of the rebate program. Pliny's concern that other estate owners correctly implemented his program further reinforced Pliny's status with the elite as a talented businessman who generously shared his knowledge and experiences.

To conclude this discussion on Pliny's motivation, we have assumed that that the order of events underlying Letter 8.2's creation was that Pliny first designed a program for compensating the buyers and the letter's subsequent publication followed a successful implementation of the rebate plan. The critical point here and why we have spent so much time discussing Pliny's motivation, is to recognize the importance of the two-step process that we have attributed to Pliny. He first implemented a successful program (whose critical steps in his rebate's design are shown in Figure 2.2) and only

2 - Pliny's Epistle 8.2

then capitalized on the program's success in order to enhance his reputation. To properly ensure that he received his due, Pliny took exquisite care in describing the program and its positive reception to Calvisius Rufus as well as his book's intended readers. This was a man determined not to lose the record of his business success to the purple mists of viticulture history.

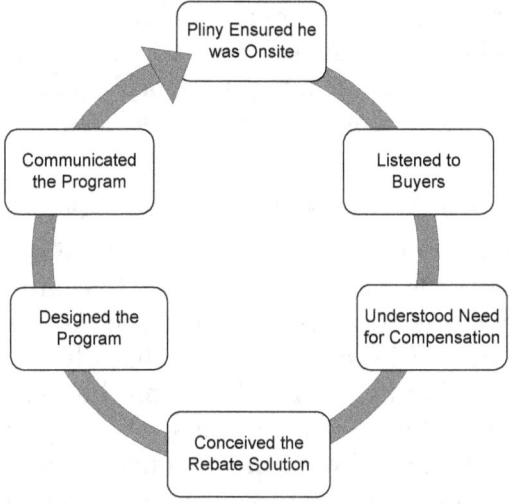

Figure 2.2: The six most critical steps in Pliny's effort to construct a successful rebate program in response to a problematic harvest.

Pliny aggressively promoted his good deeds and it is those actions, following the program's successful implementation (and perhaps influenced the letter's final construction), that brings us to our first lesson of Plinian management.

Entrepreneurship and Ethics in Ancient Rome

Lesson 1: Promote your Successes

Today, we tend to look askance at self-promotion in business, often ascribing the adjective "shameless" to the noun. Conversely, the ancient Romans actually encouraged self-promotion but only if the achievements were real. Though, there was never a shortage of self-promoters in ancient Rome (or in any period for that matter) let us examine two very different but acceptable ancient Roman examples that exhibit Pliny's demonstrated two-step process of self-promotion, (i.e. a process based upon a solid foundation of accomplishment and success.)

Supporting Example of Julius Caesar

The first supporting example for this Plinian management lesson is that of Julius Caesar during a victory parade (known as a Triumph) for a war in Asia Minor (the same province that Pliny would later help administer). In a Triumph the victorious general would be "drawn in a chariot – accompanied by the booty he had won, the prisoners he had taken captive and his no doubt rowdy and raucous troops in their battle gear – through the streets of the city (Rome)"[25] According to Suetonius, Caesar placed on one of the processional displays (somewhat similar to a parade float today) that rolled through Rome the following well known inscription: "I came, I saw, I conquered."[26] There was nothing subtle about Caesar's efforts of self-promotion here but they were absolutely built on his extraordinary history of military success.

2 - Pliny's Epistle 8.2

Figure 2.3: Shows a marble bust of Julius Caesar. Caesar's self-promotion was based on an extraordinary history of success.[27]

Supporting Example of Eurysaces the Baker and his Wife

At the other end of the social strata from Caesar and much closer to the business paradigm of Pliny, we find the ex-slave Eurysaces who lived in the time of Caesar and died near the end of the Roman Republic (circa 50-20 BC). Eurysaces was a very successful baker in ancient Rome. We know of him today because, in the modern city of Rome, his tomb still stands - an edifice as dramatic today as when it was first constructed. The tomb originally rose over 30 feet in height and, when fully unearthed in 1838, revealed an inscription that read "This

Entrepreneurship and Ethics in Ancient Rome

is the monument of Marcus Vegilius Eurysaces, baker, contractor, public servant."[28] Eurysaces was not satisfied with just building a gigantic tomb for himself; "[h]e chose a conspicuous site at a major intersection near the (ancient) city. The architectural form of the monument he put up was utterly original."[29] Eurysaces went so far as to have the design of his mausoleum resemble the baking implements of his profession and added a frieze with an image of him overseeing the baking process. There could be no mistaking his emphasis – inscription, frieze and design all reinforced his message – here for eternity lay an extremely successful baker and businessman.

Found nearby and assumed part of the funerary monument were the remains of a sculpture of a couple with the epitaph: "Atista was my wife. She lived as a wonderful woman, the remains of whose body which survive are in this breadbasket."[30] Now this is a man who took his passion for the self-promotion of his work (and his wife) to the grave and beyond!

2 - Pliny's Epistle 8.2

Figure 2.4: The tomb Eurysaces the baker had built and used for his self-promotion[31]. The Emperor Claudius appears to have incorporated the tomb into his imperial building program.

The Importance of Funerary Inscriptions

It is also important to note though that funerary inscriptions by the marginalized lower classes of Rome were very common (although not anywhere near the size and scope of Eurysaces') and were specifically intended to, "record who they were in death and in life."[32] The tomb of Eurysaces offered a freedman such as himself a unique opportunity to remove "the stain of a servile past"[33] and to promote his life's accomplishments with pride. Despite the lowly social status of Eurysaces, as the footprint of the city of Rome evolved, none of the emperors who followed the Roman Republic's fall ever demolished the ostentatious tomb of Eurysaces and the Emperor Claudius appears to have even ordered the tomb incorporated into his building program.[34] The self

Entrepreneurship and Ethics in Ancient Rome

promotion of Eurysaces, the lowly ex-slave, oddly foreshadowed in stone what Pliny's contemporary, the famous poet Juvenal, accomplished with the phrase "bread and circuses" – the immortalization of bread and its politics in ancient Rome.

Self-Promotion in the Modern Business World

With regard to his accomplishments, Pliny was unfortunately much less than a Caesar and fortunately more than a Eurysaces. But with respect to successful self-promotion, Pliny exemplified a bit of both, for while Caesar's method was to build his legacy upon his conquests and Eurysaces' ensured his notoriety through the construction of a monstrous tomb, Pliny chose to erect an eternal monument to himself via his letters.

In today's business world, the ability to build a reputation of competence still requires a solid basis of success; however, we should also not ignore Oscar Wilde's sentiment, as well demonstrated by both Caesar and Eurysaces, that "nothing succeeds like excess." This is not an argument for promotion to outstrip the success upon which it is based but rather recognition that quiet competence can often be relegated to obscurity in any business environment. In other words, quietly competent individuals will be rewarded, for they are appreciated but unfortunately they are at times overlooked in their efforts to climb the corporate ladder and, in the case of the entrepreneur, the inability to successfully, if not excessively, promote one's business can greatly retard growth.

Pliny clearly recognized that more than quiet competence was required to obtain maximum

2 - Pliny's Epistle 8.2

recognition as seen in a letter of his to the Emperor Trajan. Pliny directly requested an appointment to the pinnacle of the Roman priesthood. Trajan granted the request and must have felt it was deserved; however, the fact remains that Pliny had to ask for it first. Pliny wrote: "I pray you therefore, to add to the honours to which I have been raised by your kindness by granting me a priesthood."[35] Pliny had no misgivings about asking his superior for what he desired and in today's fast paced business environment an aspiring business professional must be prepared to do the same.

Finally, it should be noted that, as one progresses in a successful career, the potential for self-promotion increases as one's seniority increases within an organization or as one's business grows. This is because the wider the scope of responsibility, the more frequently complex issues and challenges emerge, increasing the set of self-promotion opportunities and of course increasing the potential for very visible failures. The balancing of success-based self-promotion such that it appears as something less than undue self-aggrandizement and more than quiet competence is a skill best developed over time, beginning with little more than the successful completion of the job at hand and good organizational sensitivity, combined with the careful selection of trusted advisors.

Pliny's Advisors

One trusted Pliny advisor was Calvisius Rufus, an equestrian in Pliny's home district of Comum[36] to whom Pliny addressed not just Epistle 8.2 but five other letters as well. In one of those letters,

Entrepreneurship and Ethics in Ancient Rome

Pliny shared some gossip with Calvisius Rufus as evidenced by Pliny's opening line: "Have your copper (money) ready and hear a first rate story..."[37] From this we can conclude that Calvisius Rufus was an intimate of Pliny's. Calvisius Rufus' role also included his functioning as a business consultant to Pliny. This can be seen when Pliny made the following request of Calvisius Rufus: "As usual, I am calling upon your expert advice on a matter of property."[38]

We should note that Pliny set a very high standard for his business associates as well as those he would recommend for administrative positions. Addressing an aspiring applicant's qualifications for office, Pliny wrote of the candidate: "His is the advice I follow in business ... for he is a man of exceptional sincerity, integrity and understanding."[39] We must therefore assume that Pliny felt the same about Calvisius Rufus when he selected him as his hometown's recipient of the complex details of his rebate plan. Pliny's standards in the selection of his advisors establishes for us a second Plinian management lesson.

Lesson 2: Establish Rigorous Standards for Advisors

Pliny was very selective in his choice of advisors and explicitly counseled the same caution to a another friend whom he supported for an administrative position in Egypt,[40] reminding him that "men have the same right to judge but not the same ability to judge wisely."[41] Pliny's guidance unequivocally applies to the modern business executive as well, for the failure to be judicious in one's choice of

2 - Pliny's Epistle 8.2

advisors, whether those advisors are consultants, staff, or friends, can often result in irreparable damage to both a career and a business. Even the authors of the Bible thought that care in selecting one's associates was sufficiently important for the inclusion of an admonition similar to Pliny's lesson in the Old Testament's *Book of Proverbs* (Verse 13.20): "Walk with wise men and you will become wise but the companion of fools will fare badly."[42]

Implementation Challenges

As with most wise counsel, the immediate question is how to operationalize the advice and, in this particular case, how to consistently implement the lesson. Perhaps the best approach is to go back again to the bar Pliny set for himself in the choice of advisors – choose those with sincerity, integrity and understanding but the evaluating manager must remember that sincerity resists objective measurement and integrity offers little room for measured gradations. Understanding however, can be directly correlated to competence and an advisor's competence can and should be consistently evaluated against objective, well gradated benchmarks to ensure that "walking with wise men" will be the more likely outcome than being the "the companion of fools".

Unfortunately there are those occasions when advisors fall short of the required standards and must be replaced. This often occurs when advisors fail to sufficiently grow with the rising executive or keep pace with the successful expansion of the company, thus reducing their value to the responsible manager and the company. In these

Entrepreneurship and Ethics in Ancient Rome

instances of business growth (and sometimes contraction), the executive must first re-evaluate the advisor benchmarks and then measure the incumbents against those revised benchmarks. The difficulty is that competence must ultimately trump loyalty in the decision process and this becomes especially challenging for a manager if the struggling advisor is a long-serving staff member. This often emotionally charged process is a necessary acknowledgement that an executive's ultimate loyalty must be to the success of the entire enterprise and therefore must take precedence over personal loyalties.

Advice from the Emperor Augustus

Before a final decision is made to replace an advisor, however, care must be taken to ensure that the potential successor truly offers more to the business in the long term than the incumbent. This approach was well summarized by the long ruling and deified Roman Emperor Augustus who frequently instructed his staff when making appointments: "Let's be satisfied with the Cato we have."[43] Cato was a staunch defender of the Roman Republic and chose suicide rather than submit to the dictatorship of Augustus' adoptive father, Julius Caesar. In fact, Cato's staunch defense of liberty and "final act of defiance"[44] was not only admired by generations of Romans but also by America's Founding Fathers as well. The ideals of liberty epitomized by Cato's words, deeds and death, so impressed George Washington that Washington, despite congressional prohibitions, had a play about Cato performed for his soldiers at Valley Forge.[45] Even Augustus, as Caesar's heir and the first emperor of Rome,

2 - Pliny's Epistle 8.2

recognized and acknowledged Cato's courage by his repetitive use of his quote above. The message that Augustus looked to repeatedly deliver is that it is often extremely difficult to find the ideal candidate and that an executive just might need to be satisfied with the "Cato" on hand. This advice should be carefully weighed before replacing an incumbent to ensure that the result is truly worth the effort.

An additional Piece of Plinian Advice

Pliny made an important additional point with relevance to the identification of competence and although he was referring to literary talent, the advice serves us here as well: "there are men who may be rustic in appearance but are found on closer inspection to be well armed and equipped and full of spirit and fire."[46] This counsel of Pliny's predates our well-known 20th century phrase "don't judge a book by its cover" by over eighteen centuries.

Pliny's Modes of Communication

As we discussed earlier, Calvisius Rufus was from Pliny's home district of Comum and was not local to the estate where Pliny implemented his rebate program, so he would not have been aware of Pliny's accomplishments with the rebates unless so informed by Pliny. Therefore, if Pliny desired to share the steps he had undertaken and to have word spread about the plan within his home district, a letter to Calvisius Rufus was an excellent means for doing so; it would have allowed Calvisius Rufus to spread the word of Pliny's successful actions on Pliny's behalf without Pliny appearing to be unduly self-serving in the process. The dissemination of

Entrepreneurship and Ethics in Ancient Rome

Pliny's success on his Tuscan estates to a wider audience than his home district required another means of distributing the letter and including Letter 8.2 among his published correspondence successfully accomplished this goal. Pliny's utilization of the communications channels available to him at the time (locally perhaps by word of mouth, in his home district by letter and to his circle of friends and peers via the publication of his books) brings us to our third lesson of Plinian Management.

Lesson 3: Align the Message with the Medium

In Pliny's time, as noted above, there were extremely limited means of communications for sharing lessons of successful (or unsuccessful) personal endeavors. Often a friend or a traveler heading in the direction of the recipient's locale would simply carry a note or letter to the intended recipient. This is seen in the correspondence of Cicero, writing from Rome and complaining to his close friend Atticus in Athens that "Letters from you reach me all too seldom, though travelers to Rome are much easier for you to come by than travelers to Athens for me."[47] Even if there were available travelers, they were not always reliable, as we hear from Cicero, who was away from Rome and again complaining to his patient friend Atticus: "As usual, I was avidly expecting a letter from you towards evening, when along comes word that some boys have arrived from Rome. I call them in and ask whether they have any letters for me. They say not. 'What', say I, 'nothing from Pomponius (Atticus)?' Frightened by my tone and look they confessed that they had been given one but had lost it on the way."[48] Cicero, like Pliny, could always send one of his slaves as a special courier but that would have required exceptional circumstances that ordinary communications typically did not warrant.

Imperial Communication

In the case of the emperor's business, there was an imperial postal system in use for letters and/or authorized individuals to improve speed and reliability. In fact, the use of the imperial post was important enough that Pliny wrote multiple times to the Emperor Trajan specifically about the post's use while he was serving in Bithynia as the emperor's special envoy. The first instance appears almost trivial (further supporting the view that Pliny was somewhat obsessed with details) and was regarding expired post permits. Pliny enquired of the Emperor about their use: "Are permits to use the Imperial Post valid after their date has expired and, if so, for how long?"[49] It should be noted, however, that the question was not so trivial that Trajan failed to respond.

In another instance, Pliny had authorized his wife to use the Imperial Post for travel during a family emergency and Pliny apologetically wrote to the Emperor: "Up to now, Sir, I have made it a fixed rule not to issue anyone a permit to use the Imperial Post unless he is traveling on your service but I have just been obliged to make an exception ... and I felt sure that you would approve of a journey made for family reasons."[50] The correspondence above reveals just how important Trajan viewed the imperial postal system to his governance. The systems' continued existence under a succession of emperors clearly demonstrated both the need and desire for timely information as well as the existence of a means for the relatively rapid propagation of that information, although one typically denied all but the emperor.[51]

Time Sensitivity of Communication

The information contained in Pliny's Letter 8.2 was complex but not particularly time sensitive (especially given that it was probably written after both the harvest and Pliny's return to Rome) and, even if it were, would still have been relegated to some form of casual posting. Upon Calvisius Rufus' receipt, despite any delays in its transmission, Pliny's hometown neighbors would still reap the benefit of his counsel whenever they felt they needed to apply a rebate to their partners once they learned of the content of Pliny's letter. This could have been easily accomplished by the letter's "circulation or reading in an open forum,"[52] perhaps with a further commentary offered by Calvisius Rufus. For the readers of Pliny's published letters, the program's description would have had to stand completely on its own and for that reason Pliny may have felt the need to redact the letter with the added calculation example to ensure clarity. However, we should also note that the original letter to Calvisius Rufus might simply have contained the example to help assure Pliny of Calvisius Rufus' comprehension of the rebate program.

2 - Pliny's Epistle 8.2

Modern Dissemination of "Best Practices"

Today, we have a multiplicity of communication technologies that affords us the luxury of both sharing business information instantaneously as well as customizing the content and format with any level of complexity acceptable to the medium chosen from tweets to video. Companies have also even established formal methods to share successful approaches to problem resolution or innovative techniques. What Pliny intended with Epistle 8.2 has evolved into a standard process that today is better known by the business buzzwords "best practices." We should also note that the dissemination of a best practice affords the best practice's creator a formal opportunity to craft and communicate a personal or team success story facilitating an officially sanctioned opportunity for self-promotion without the unpleasant scent of self-interest.

Chapter Conclusion

In this chapter, we have seen that Pliny, with his publication of a successful business practice, worked hard to avoid, with questionable success, the criticism that has dogged Pliny's hero Cicero throughout history. That criticism, according to the ancient Roman historian and biographer Plutarch, (another Pliny contemporary,) was that Cicero "filled his books and writings with his own praises, to such an excess as to render a style, in itself most pleasant and delightful, nauseous and irksome to his hearers, this ungrateful humour like a disease, always cleaving to him."[53] In Epistle 8.2, Pliny avoided the odor of blatant self-promotion and did so by fully recognizing the need to carefully craft his message to the communication medium available to him at the time.

We also have seen that Pliny clearly understood the value of his rebate program and looked to disseminate, via the means available to him, his "best practice" contained in Epistle 8.2 to a wider audience: first to the grape buyers (and most likely) his neighbors proximate to his Tuscan estate next to his confidant Calvisius Rufus and the neighbors of his Comum estate and then finally to the readers of his book. From Pliny's artful construction of Epistle 8.2, the thoughtful selection of his correspondent and his successful dissemination of the content of his letter, three lessons of Plinian Management have been identified and discussed:

- Lesson 1: Promote your Successes
- Lesson 2: Establish Rigorous Standards for Advisors
- Lesson 3: Align the Message with the Medium

CHAPTER 3

Pliny's Business Problem

Before describing the business problem he faced, Pliny began Letter 8.2, as we saw earlier, with an opening bit of casual banter to Calvisius Rufus about the financial challenges with which he constantly wrestled and claimed to have consistently lost:

> "Other people visit their estates to come away richer than before but I go only to return the poorer."

Pliny's use of humor here allowed him to accomplish three goals. First, the self-deprecation offered a sense of intimacy with Calvisius Rufus and other readers and reaffirmed their social bond. Second, Pliny's self-deprecation would also have disarmed a reader, establishing a gentle counteraction to the self-promotion that followed. Third and perhaps most importantly, Pliny's jocular lament about being "poorer" could only have strengthened the perception of the generosity of Pliny's later solution.

Entrepreneurship and Ethics in Ancient Rome

To be generous in the face of financial reverses trumps generosity in good times. So, even while self-deprecating in his opening sentence, Pliny was again subtly self-promoting but under the guise of casual humor. Clearly, Pliny learned well from his teacher, Quintilian, who taught that certain forms of humor:

> "steal(s) into the minds of men in a peculiar manner and which is extremely pleasing when it is well managed."[54]

This careful use of humor brings us to a fourth lesson of Plinian Management.

Lesson 4: Self-Deprecate in Difficult Situations

The opening sentence of this letter is not a unique instance of Pliny's use of humor when discussing his supposed financial hardships from a harvest. In another letter to a literary acquaintance, Pliny remarked:

> "I have the same (bad) news from my farms, so I shall have time, too, to write ... so long as I can still afford to buy paper."[55]

Pliny was also not alone in using self-deprecation when discussing his business challenges. Cicero, Pliny's role model in most endeavors, did so as well. In a letter from Cicero to the ever-patient Atticus, Cicero wrote of the status of one of his real estate investments:

> "Two of my shops have collapsed and the others are showing cracks, so that even the mice have moved elsewhere, to say nothing of the tenants."[56]

3 - Pliny's Business Problem

Cicero here revealed a bit more comedic skill than Pliny typically could muster, especially given the date of Cicero's letter – April 17, 44 BC – just over a month after the Ides of March and the assassination of Julius Caesar.

To laugh in the face of a difficult situation is a virtue as long as the seriousness of that situation is properly dealt with and not treated as a triviality. Pliny the orator, like Cicero, would have well understood that an audience enjoys and often requires, a laugh in difficult or tense times. The use of humor has the additional benefit of allowing one to showcase the capability to face adversity with clarity and without undue concern or distress. Therefore, wit is quite a useful tool but one that is not always essential or appropriate so it must be used with care. When wit does not apply, calm competence, if it can be managed, is typically a very acceptable alternative.

Pliny as a Hands-on Executive

We are, however, still unfinished with Pliny's first sentence. Self-deprecating humor aside, Pliny makes another critical point. He said, with respect to his estate, "I go". In other words, Pliny makes it very clear that he was on site supervising and thus in control of the decision-making process. This hands-on approach is reinforced in another later letter of Pliny's when he was working directly for the Emperor Trajan and he wrote to the Emperor requesting some time off to deal with ongoing agricultural difficulties. Pliny specifically informed Trajan that:

Entrepreneurship and Ethics in Ancient Rome

> *"the series of bad harvests we have had are forcing me to consider reducing (tenant) rents and I cannot calculate these unless I am on the spot"*[57]

Pliny needed to be "on the spot" to address the issues at hand. So, as in our letter here, it was important that Pliny be physically on site and personally involved in the problem's resolution. As we saw earlier, in antiquity, information about one's estate could be transported only as fast as an individual could travel: by foot, horse, or ship. If possible, the best alternative was to be on site and not have to wait for the receipt of a letter or verbal report.

Harvest time is a crucial time for any farmer and clearly Pliny placed himself at his estate when it was both necessary and feasable. Since crops require time to mature it is likely that Pliny was alerted by letter in advance of the harvest to potential problems with the grape crop. Feasibility of travel has to be considered as well, not only from the perspective of Pliny's availability (he had many interests and responsibilities) but also due to both the duration of time required to be on site as well as the length of time any trip to and from the estate would require. For instance, in the letter to Trajan above, Pliny went on to write,

> *"I cannot manage with less than a month, as the town and farms I am talking about are more than 150 miles from Rome."*[58]

A visit by Pliny to the Tuscan estate discussed in Letter 8.2 must have been scheduled and planned well in advance whereas a visit during an emergency may simply have been physically impossible. Pliny

3 - Pliny's Business Problem

mentioned just such an emergency situation at the same Tuscan estate when he wrote in 104/105AD[59]:

> "I hear that hail has done a lot of damage to my property in Tuscany"[60]

Obviously Pliny was not at this property during the storm, which would have been devastating to the grapes on the vine. This can be assumed as the case since in this same letter he further elaborated that a second estate's crop was good but prices were low and that he had only one other estate "to bring me in anything."[61] There was no humor in this situation and, despite the devastation, Pliny did not travel to deal with the crisis. Thus, Pliny must have relied on his bailiff to handle the emergency and given his multiple estates, we can assume that in other instances, Pliny was forced to rely upon others to manage through the difficulties. Clearly, travel to a remote estate required advance planning unless there was an emergency so dire, such as the illness or death of a family member, that travel was commenced immediately, as we saw above when Pliny had a family emergency (the death of his wife's grandfather) and utilized the Imperial Post without authorization from the Emperor.

In the case of his visit to his Tuscan property described in Letter 8.2, related letters indicate[62] that Pliny undertook an extended tour of the Tuscan region around harvest time. It could have been a coincidence but the most likely scenario was that Pliny was aware well in advance of his trip that there would be issues with the season's harvest due either to market or climate conditions and that he wanted to deal with the problems personally (as well as take the opportunity to see some "natural curiosities"[63]). Therefore, from Pliny's initial opening jocular sentence, we are able to extract a second management lesson relating to problem diagnosis and resolution during a period of business turmoil.

Lesson 5: Manage Crises in Person

As Pliny's letters have shown, during difficult periods (as in the case of the poor harvest or tenant arrears), there was no substitute for real time and accurate information gained through personal involvement. Even in the tumultuous months preceding Julius Caesar's death, the perpetually preoccupied Cicero wrote Atticus:

> "I must go to Arpinum. My little properties there need my attention and I am afraid I may not be able to get away once Caesar comes home."[64]

Balancing Hands-on Management and Delegation

Pliny's and Cicero's examples reveal the need at times to manage in person but in no way are intended to insist that one must always be in the middle of every business crisis, managing onsite. On the contrary, both men's correspondence reveals that they did not shy away from assigning work to others. This is seen by Pliny's delegation of authority for the purchase of a statuary plinth "Choose what marble you like"[65] and in his request for the purchase of temple columns in his home district: "Will you then please buy me four marble columns, any kind you think suitable."[66] Cicero, too, delegated construction work to an associate (a businessman

3 - Pliny's Business Problem

named Vestorius) in the case of the collapsing shops mentioned earlier, as seen when Cicero commented to Atticus: "there is a building scheme under way, Vestorius advising and investigating, which should turn this loss into a source of profit."[67]

However, it is important to note that none of these construction examples involved significant problems and, although the earlier example of the hail damage to Pliny's estate was potentially serious, Pliny most likely chose not to travel because it was already too late to do anything, as the damage was done. It was also possible that he was preoccupied with other more serious business or that he simply had faith in his bailiff to respond properly and handle the situation. Pliny and Cicero basically had only two solutions for managing a business crisis: intervene personally or have a designee do so, since there was no other reliable means to manage in real-time.

Today, we have reliable means to manage a crisis remotely and in real-time, providing the responsible executive the luxury of deciding precisely at which point remote management should give way to an onsite presence: at the beginning, end, or any time in between, the failure to choose the correct time for personal intervention, however, can derail a career almost as often as the failure to successfully address the crisis at hand. "Too soon" an appearance hints of micro-managing and poor recruitment of staff, while "too late" is indicative of remoteness and failure to be sufficiently hands-on.

Entrepreneurship and Ethics in Ancient Rome

The Importance of Accurate Information in a Crisis

Finally, the inability to obtain accurate information throughout a crisis often can result in a misunderstanding of the problem at hand and dramatically complicate the identification of a solution. As we saw above, Pliny and Cicero could only obtain their real-time information through direct personal involvement. Modern communication technology can seduce a crisis manager into remote management but that executive must remain extraordinarily vigilant to the reliability and accuracy of the information provided. Far too often, members of crisis management teams have understated the size and scope of a crisis, provided less than accurate data, or sought to protect their own careers, creating additional complications for the executive charged with the resolution of the crisis. These same problems may still arise even if an executive is onsite but they typically would be more quickly recognized and more easily dealt with via personal intervention than with remote management.

Pliny's Problem Detailed

Fortunately for Pliny (and for us), he was onsite for the harvest of 107 AD and, as a result, addressed the crisis in person but then claimed he was the poorer because of it. Understanding why this occurred brings us to the core of Pliny's business problem. In fact, Pliny wasted no time in describing his problem, for he immediately followed his lighthearted opening sentence in the letter with a description of the

3 - Pliny's Business Problem

situation that evolved between him and his grape buyers. Pliny reported in this portion of Epistle 8.2:

"I had sold my grape harvest to the dealers who were eager to buy when the price quoted at the time was tempting and prospects seemed good. Their hopes were frustrated."

These two sentences indicate that the grape dealers committed to or paid a price for the harvest early in the season when "they were eager" and they were now disappointed with the transaction. Since Pliny specifically referenced "tempting" price quotes and failed to say that the harvest was poor, we must assume that the problem was not with the harvest itself, for usually Pliny is not shy about complaining of a poor harvest as we saw earlier and again with another harvest when he reported "the grape harvest, which is poor but better than I had expected."[68] If the grape harvest of 107 AD were poor, Pliny would have reported that fact to Calvisius Rufus. Therefore, given what Pliny wrote about the price quotes and what he did not say about the harvest, we can infer that the problem was not with the harvest itself but rather with the price of the grapes (likely due to an overabundant crop of grapes causing a glut on the market). In other words, we would report today that the market for grapes had weakened and the prices had fallen or had even collapsed[69]. The New York Times ran just such a story in 2003 on the collapse of grape prices entitled: "California Grape Rush of 90s Withers as Prices Collapse."[70] Clearly a period of falling grape prices was not unique to Pliny's era.

Entrepreneurship and Ethics in Ancient Rome

Background on the Selling of Grapes on the Vine

Before we examine Pliny's specific transaction with the grape dealers and the grape price collapse that created his problem, let us take a look at the practice of dealers buying grapes on the vine in ancient Rome. Writing nearly a quarter of a millennium before Pliny, the great-grandfather of the Cato discussed earlier, Cato the Elder, an early Roman statesmen and author, wrote extensively of the practice of selling grapes in advance of the harvest and even detailed the recommended terms of sale in his book, *On Agriculture*.[71] We see that Pliny was following a well-established tradition amongst landowners to sell their grapes on the vine to dealers who bought the forthcoming harvest effectively "on spec." Discussing a harvest of grapes much closer to Pliny's time, his uncle, Pliny the Elder, wrote of what must have been considered a very large example of selling grapes on the vine to a single dealer:

> "the vintage, while still hanging on the trees, was knocked down to a purchaser at a price of 400,000 sesterces."[72]

The Risks and Opportunities for the Grape Buyers

Purchasing the grape crop on the vine posed market, horticultural and climatological risks but must have still offered significant profit opportunities, since there appears to have been no shortage of buyers for grapes on the vine. The practice endured for centuries and with what appears to be a perpetual

3 - Pliny's Business Problem

availability of "hundreds upon hundreds of wine merchants."[73] The risks and rewards for just such a dealer and his personality, are described in an unvarnished character sketch by the author Petronius, whom is often assumed to be the Petronius described by Tacitus as an intimate of the Emperor Nero chosen to serve "as a critic in matters of taste."[74] In his work of satirical fiction, *The Satyricon,* Petronius colorfully described a recently deceased wine dealer:

> "That boy would have grubbed in the gutter for a coin and picked it out with his teeth too ... a regular pair of fists on legs ... what does our boy do but flop on his first big deal ... But come the vintage and he got right back on his feet and sold his wine at his own figure."[75]

Petronius' description is perhaps no surprise, as we would expect these dealers to have had the toughness to negotiate with some of Rome's most powerful and wealthy landowners, as well as an iron gut to stomach the annual vagaries of the grape harvest, betting on vintages months in advance. This was clearly not a profession for the meek!

The Opportunities and Risks for Pliny

Now that we have a better understanding of the buyers, we should ask "What of the nature of the sellers? Why would Pliny choose to sell his harvest in this fashion?" Erdkamp, in his economic study of ancient Rome's grain market, offers two complementary and insightful reasons. First, by employing the grape dealers, a seller such as Pliny would have "avoided close involvement in the

Entrepreneurship and Ethics in Ancient Rome

processing and marketing of these crops."[76] The appeal here for Pliny or any other large landowner is similar to that of any company today – outsource that which is nonstrategic to reduce investment, complexity and/or risk.

Even in antiquity, there was a multiplicity of complex steps required to pick grapes and then produce, store, transport and market wine. Why incur the labor costs, the risk of weak prices, a poor harvest, or shipments lost at sea when one could simply sell the grapes on the vine? Pliny the Elder again provides an example, perhaps a bit tongue in cheek,[77] of a risk in the picking process in southern Italy:

> *"In Campania the vines espouse the poplars and embracing their brides and climbing with wanton arms ... soaring aloft to such a height that a hired vintager expressly stipulates in his contract for the cost of a funeral and a grave!"*[78]

Petronius in his *Satyricon* also provides an example of the potential risks in the later stages of the wine trade. Through the words of his buffoonish character, Trimalchio, an ex-slave with obscene wealth (often assumed to be modeled on Eurysaces[79]), we learn of the risks inherent in the transport of wine. Trimalchio brags to his guests at a dinner:

> *"I had five ships built. Then I stocked them with wine ... worth its weight in gold at the time – and shipped them off to Rome. ...(All) five (were) wrecked."*[80]

3 - Pliny's Business Problem

Exaggeration aside, there were many risks in the wine business to be navigated and Pliny most likely selected to sell his grapes on the vine (a practice not uncommon to Rome's elite) in order to simplify the work for which his estate was responsible and to minimize the risks associated with the harvesting and selling of his grape crop.

We should note that the practice of selling a grape crop in advance of the harvest and locking in the price before the harvest continues to the present time. A 2011 survey[81] of 168 grape growers and grower-vintners revealed that 58% of the respondents had sold more than half their crop in advance of the harvest (see Figure 3.1).

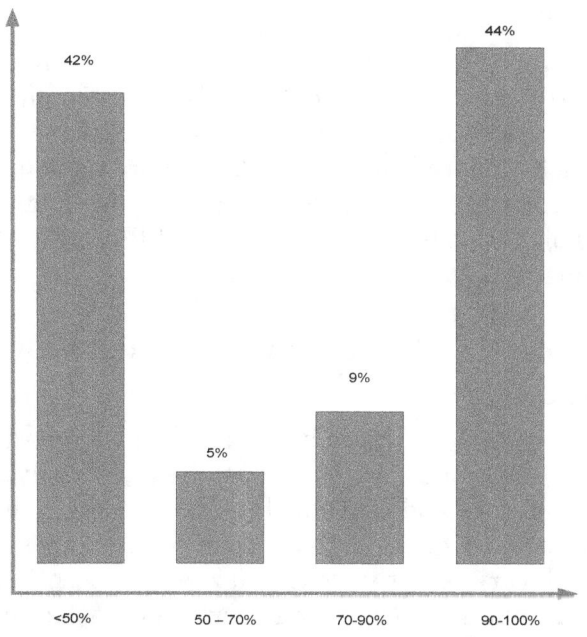

Figure 3.1: The results of a 2011 survey of 168 growers and grower/vintners indicate that the practice of reducing risk by selling one's grapes in advance of the harvest has continued to the present day. (Chart courtesy of BPM Wine)

Entrepreneurship and Ethics in Ancient Rome

The Economics of Pliny Selling his Grapes on the Vine

The second reason provided by Erdkamp focuses on the economics of the transaction between Pliny and the grape buyers. Erdkamp argues that:

> "The transaction between Pliny and the merchants who bought the grapes before the harvest implies that each of the parties was driven by opposite considerations. The merchants acted upon the expectation that the price difference in time would offer them a profit. Pliny discarded the opportunity to make a larger profit in the future and accepted the sum offered before the future market price was known."[82]

It should be no surprise from all we have seen of Pliny so far that he would be risk averse and prefer to lock in a fixed price early in order to avoid the risks inherent in a season's crop production in general and with grape growing in particular. This brings us to another example of Plinian Management.

Lesson 6: Fully Evaluate Transactional Risks

Pliny's opting for the safe harbor of an advanced sale for the harvest of 107 AD, a path he most likely had chosen before and continued to utilize going forward from the date of his Letter 8.2, shows a business outlook very sensitive to the risk of a transaction. Given Pliny's wealth, it can be argued that he could well have afforded to assume and absorb greater risk but it would appear out of character for Pliny to

3 - Pliny's Business Problem

accept undue risk despite the potential for improved returns.

An Example Pliny's Evaluation of Risk

An excellent example of Pliny's thought process when dealing with risk is seen in the same letter in which Pliny earlier solicited Calvisius Rufus' expert advice. The opinion required was with regard to the potential purchase of an estate bordering his Tuscan property with a sale price marked down (for crop yield and production issues) from HS 5 million to HS 3 million, an amount that would have been significant even for the wealthy Pliny. We must assume, since Pliny requested input from Calvisius Rufus, that a response from his advisor to his enquiry would have been an important additional element of Pliny's risk/reward calculation.

To assist Calvisius Rufus in his evaluation, Pliny proceeded to carefully define in his letter the pros and cons of the transaction that he was considering. Pliny wrote:

> "The estate joining my own is for sale ... The primary attraction is the obvious amenity if the properties were joined ... (I could) visit the two without making more than one journey ... Both could be put under the same steward and practically the same foreman ... On the other hand I am afraid it may be rash to expose a property of such a size to the same uncertainties of weather and general risks ... it might be safer to meet the hazards of fortune by having estates in different localities."[83]

Entrepreneurship and Ethics in Ancient Rome

Pliny's Concern for the Unexpected

Pliny was unsurprisingly methodical in documenting his evaluation of the rewards and the risks associated with completing this real estate transaction, although we should note there was no financial detail (perhaps redacted out) regarding the required investments to improve the estate, no mention of a rate of return on his total expected investment, nor any discussion of the payback period. Pliny instead emphasized his concern with unpredictability call it luck or fortune which can never be controlled or forecast but on which Pliny, like most Romans, was clearly focused. Pliny further revealed his exquisite sensitivity to the impact of fortune in a letter to a former equestrian officer who served under him.[84] Pliny warned: "be sure of nothing, when we see so many fluctuations of fortune."[85]

Elsewhere, Pliny noted that not just fortune could affect one's outcome when he advised that "often a mere touch is enough to set things moving with far-reaching consequences."[86] Today, Pliny's comment of the impact of a "mere touch" would be comfortably ensconced in modern chaos theory, which studies the impact of small initial perturbations on major events and, in business, as in life, sometimes the least regarded of decisions can snowball into the largest of unanticipated problems. The modern business executive, like Pliny, must always understand that, despite all the detailed planning, there is always an element of risk, bad luck, or an unseen gentle touch to conspire against those plans.

3 - Pliny's Business Problem

Pliny's Risk/Reward Calculus

Given our understanding of Pliny's concerns for the risks of the real estate transaction, its cost and potential rewards, we are in a position to gain insight into Pliny's risk/reward calculus. Although we lack the detailed financial information associated with Pliny's delineated risks and the rewards, we do know that the overall transaction price was significant. We also know the price was reduced for crop yield issues and the potential synergies Pliny anticipated by joining this estate with one he already owned. With this information in hand we can create four potential risk/reward scenarios that could describe the transaction as seen by Pliny:

1. Low Risk/Low Reward
2. Low Risk/High Reward
3. High Risk/Low Reward
4. High Risk/High Reward

Given the large purchase price, we can immediately dismiss scenarios one and two since the cost was significant even for Pliny. In fact, Pliny was sufficiently concerned to have sought advice from Calvisius Rufus on the deal. We can also dismiss scenario three since it is not likely that Pliny, who was risk averse, would have accepted the high risk associated with such a purchase price for a low reward. Thus we are left with scenario four, an option involving high risk but also a likely expectation of a high reward from the transaction as well. Pliny must have believed that he could sufficiently improve the estate's production capabilities and gain significant synergies as well so that the rewards would have eventually exceeded the risks or he likely would have not pursued the purchase.

This type of risk/reward analysis, where potential risks are compared to the potential rewards can be done graphically as shown in Figure 3.2 below. This form of graphical presentation, known as Quadrant Analysis, provides a straightforward means of comparing and selecting among multiple transactions (although we only have one in this case). Also, when the analytical data is available, Quadrant Analysis facilitates the development of strategies to reduce risks and improve rewards; for example, this approach is often utilized in portfolio management and asset acquisition where the measurement of risks and rewards is more easily quantified.

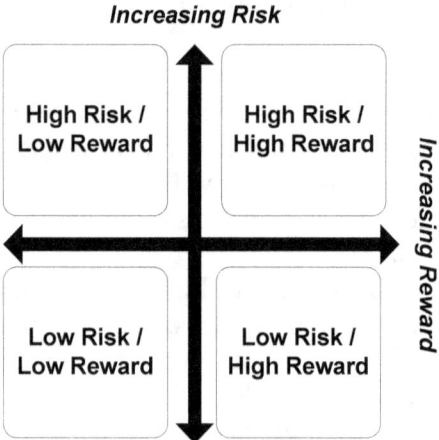

Figure 3.2: Pliny's potential risk/reward scenarios are depicted here via Quadrant Analysis, which facilitates the development of risk mitigation and reward enhancement strategies.

3 - Pliny's Business Problem

Insight into Pliny's Decision Making

Pliny's analysis for Calvisius Rufus reveals much about Pliny's very modern approach to his decision making process, his concerns with risks and his strategy for increasing the value of his potential purchase. We can assume Pliny believed that future production, the benefits of proximity to an existing estate of his, and the fact that the historical price was substantially reduced outweighed the risks, in order to justify his interest in the property and his ultimate purchase of the estate.[87] These insights are indeed helpful in understanding Pliny's approach to dealing with his grape buyers.

Now let us return (after our rather substantial digression on Pliny's approach to risk management) to the two sentences that we began analyzing earlier, examining their operational implications.

"I had sold my grape harvest to the dealers who were eager to buy when the price quoted at the time was tempting and prospects seemed good. Their hopes were frustrated."

A key word in Radice's translation above is "dealers" – plural. Pliny clearly had chosen multiple dealers rather than a single large one. Perhaps this was due to the absence of any sufficiently large player in the area or, more likely, Pliny may have intentionally divided up the area for bid so that the harvest would have been split among a number of players, in this instance his "eager buyers." Whether by choice or necessity, the concept of having a number of buyers for the harvest establishes the next management lesson from Pliny.

Entrepreneurship and Ethics in Ancient Rome

Lesson 7: Avoid Single Sourcing

The selection of a single buyer may initially seem to simplify administrative processes associated with any transaction because there is only one party to deal with in all aspects of a relationship (bidding, negotiating, contracting if required, production, payment, etc.) and that one large player may offer the best terms due to the transaction's size. However, a single source (or buyer, as in Pliny's situation) is also by definition a single point of failure. Therefore, consideration must always be given to establishing a balance between complexity, which increases with the vendor count (see Figure 3.3) and the risk, which decreases with the vendor count (see Figure 3.4).

Pliny Chose the Complexity of Multiple Vendors

In Pliny's case, if he had only selected one buyer and that buyer failed to perform for any reason whatsoever, Pliny would have been left with a harvest on the vine and no access to his markets. Thus we see that Pliny avoided the risk of that potential problem by accepting some additional complexity and maintaining multiple partners (the number of which we cannot be certain).

3 - Pliny's Business Problem

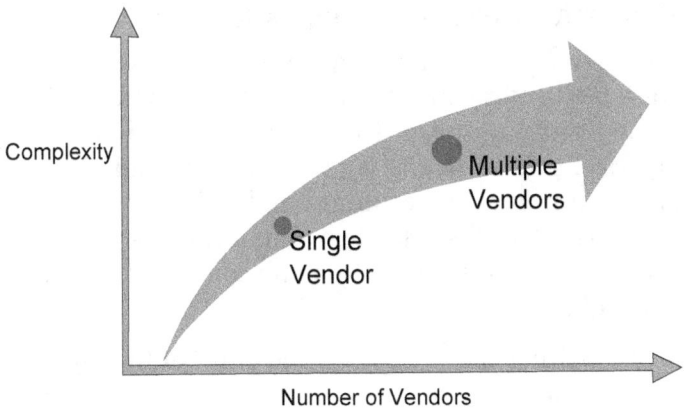

Figure 3.3: Vendor management complexity increases with the number of vendors utilized.

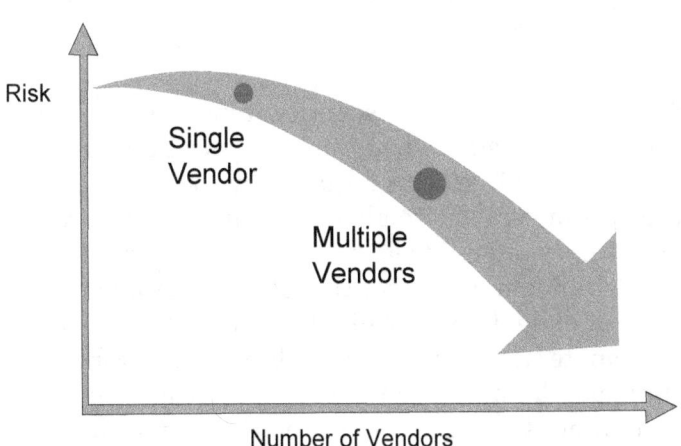

Figure 3.4: Vendor management risk decreases with the number of vendors utilized.

Entrepreneurship and Ethics in Ancient Rome

Alternative Selling Strategies for Pliny

There were alternative grape crop selling strategies[88] available to Pliny and these would have potentially yielded a greater profit than utilizing multiple buyers of grapes on the vine but they would also have required more resources and risk. These alternatives are listed below and, in Figure 3.5, are illustrated in layers of increasing complexity, risk and profit:

- Selling the grapes at "the gate" of his estate to traders;
- Transporting the grapes to town for direct sale;
- Transporting the grapes to town to sell to reselling merchants;
- Producing wine on the estate and reselling the product.

For Pliny, however, the security (remember that we have already established that he was risk averse) and limited investment required by the use of multiple buyers outweighed any surrendered profit opportunity offered from these alternate strategies. We also should not forget that Pliny's "social and political obligations left him little opportunity to participate ... directly in the selling of his crops."[89] Pliny just did not have the time (or perhaps the inclination) to go direct to his potential markets and, therefore, he willingly traded off increased profit opportunities for reduced risk and resource requirements.

3 - Pliny's Business Problem

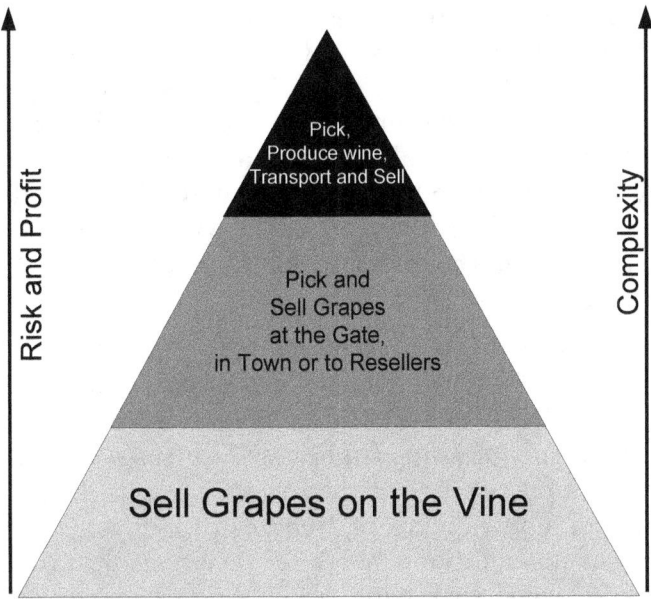

Figure 3.5: Pliny had alternative grape selling options but his resource and time requirements would have increased with each option layered above the selling of grapes on the vine. It is likely however, that Pliny's profit potential as well as his risks would have also increased with each layer.

The Marketing Strategy of the "Garum King"

An excellent example of an ancient entrepreneur without the political burdens of a Pliny who did go direct to his markets and avoided the threat of a single point of distribution failure, was the "garum king of Pompeii." Garum was an extremely popular ancient Roman fish sauce that Pliny the Elder described as:

> "consisting of the guts of fish and other parts that would otherwise be considered refuse; these are soaked in salt, so that garum is really liquor from the putrefaction of these matters."[90]

75

Entrepreneurship and Ethics in Ancient Rome

Despite its enticing description, the market for these aged, liquefied fish entrails was huge across the empire. The assumption of garum's popularity in general and the significant share of the local market exercised by Pompeii's garum king in particular are well supported by archeological evidence found in Pompeii, where there was, "the widespread distribution of the distinctive local fish sauce container."[91]

These containers often had hand painted labels and "28% of all inscribed fish sauce containers found in Pompeii and nearby Herculaneum" were linked to the family of Aulus Umbricius Scaurus – the garum king. Scaurus "either owned or controlled through family members, freedmen, or slaves, perhaps >6 additional shops in the city."[92] Scaurus clearly avoided being limited by a single source of distribution to his market and also apparently was familiar with the power of self-promotion as demonstrated by his container-branding program – an example of which is pictured on the mosaic in 3.6 and translated as: "The flower of garum, made of mackerel, a product of Scaurus, from the shop of Scaurus"[93].

3 - Pliny's Business Problem

Figure 3.6: A mosaic of Scaurus' well branded garum container.[44] *(Photo by Claus Ableiter)*

Pliny's Vendor Management Approach

Pliny eschewed the direct distribution of his grapes to the market but, as a strategy to avoid a single point of failure, he chose to utilize multiple buyers of grapes on the vine. Although this approach was less profitable than selling direct, it was also less risky and yet still accomplished the same end – the successful sale of his grapes. Pliny avoided the modern mantra of determining "a single throat to choke" which can often seduce a business executive into a false sense of security since there is a single and easily-identifiable player responsible when problems arise. But that same unitary throat offers no backup option if there is a catastrophic failure. There is obviously more work to managing multiple

Entrepreneurship and Ethics in Ancient Rome

throats in a crisis but that multiplicity of players avoids a single point of failure and has the added benefit of maintaining competition amongst the partners which we discuss next in Lesson 8.

Pliny and Vendor Contracting

In the same sentence discussing the dealers, Pliny next describes them as: "eager to buy when the price quoted at the time was tempting and prospects seemed good." Interestingly, the lawyer Pliny makes no mention of a contract in this letter that might have defined the terms of purchase of the harvest. Even as far back as Cato the Elder in his *On Agriculture*, there was a recognized need for a contract as demonstrated by Cato's instructions to his readers: "Sign a contract and give bond to the satisfaction of the owner that such payment will be made in good faith."[95] In this letter of Pliny's, there is no reference to a contract, therefore, we can only assume that Pliny simply chose not to mention its existence or that practice and Pliny's history with the buyers precluded the need for a written contract. Regardless, Pliny's comment on the "price quoted" would seem to indicate that there must still have been a formal process where terms were submitted by or negotiated with the proposed buyers and a final selection made by Pliny or possibly his bailiff. This process brings us to our next lesson in Plinian Management.

3 - Pliny's Business Problem

Lesson 8: Encourage Competition Amongst Partners

Please note that the term partners here represents Pliny's buyers. In general, partners span the business spectrum from resellers to suppliers. Based on our utilization of the translation by Radice, it is unclear whether the "price quoted" varied across Pliny's buyers. We should note that a translation by Erdkamp in this instance reads "the merchants who were eager to purchase it (the grapes on the vine), encouraged by the price it then bore."[96] Erdkamp's translation indicates that Pliny sold the harvest to multiple vendors at a fixed price – a much simpler and less competitive process than managing varying prices across multiple vendors.

Jean Andreau, in his *Banking and Business in the Ancient World,* argues for another interpretation that the process of the sale, was in fact, an auction.[97] The idea of engendering competition from multiple buyers through an auction was certainly not uncommon in ancient Rome and, although, plausible, it would appear that such a mechanism might be too untidy and disordered for Pliny's taste. Again, relying on Petronius and *The Satyricon,* we have one of the more unique descriptions of an impending auction. A minor character in the novel was once wealthy and now nearly bankrupt – an undertaker who is concerned that his creditors will get wind of his financial reversals, especially if they learn he is trying to raise money by selling his furniture at auction. The undertaker advertised for his auction in the following fashion:

"GAIUS JULIUS PROCULUS WILL HOLD AN AUCTION OF HIS SPARE FURNITURE!"[98]

Entrepreneurship and Ethics in Ancient Rome

The undertaker was looking to maintain control of the process and obtain the maximum value for what he was placing up for sale. The auction format ensured the accomplishment of this goal, as the generation of competing bids was key to maximizing the value of the furniture sold. It is, however, difficult to see a man of Pliny's stature and nature operating in this mode annually to sell his grapes.

Regardless of the precise mechanism utilized by Pliny to sell his grapes, to ultimately be successful, an auction or bid process must have sufficient bidders to produce genuine buyer competition, should be held at the most propitious time (the "dealers were eager") and the items sold placed in the best light (e.g. avoid the smell of a fire sale). So despite the scholarly disagreement over the specific format of the sale, the concept expressed here still reinforces Pliny's lesson of encouraging competition among partners.

Pliny's Attentiveness to Partner Concerns

Now we move on to the second sentence of Pliny's articulation of the difficulty at hand: "Their hopes were frustrated." What is critical in this sentence is the fact that Pliny unquestionably understood the issue at hand, perhaps even by having learned firsthand (since he was on site) of the impact of the disappointing grape prices on the merchants. We can make this important assumption since Pliny, on a number of occasions, discusses time spent listening to the complaints arising on his Tuscan estate. In one letter describing how he spent his summer days in Tuscany, Pliny wrote: "I also give some time to my tenants (they think it should be more)"[99] and,

3 - Pliny's Business Problem

in another, Pliny reveals his frustration with the complaints but also his grudging commitment to personally review all the petitions. Pliny wrote (note the self-deprecation):

> *"I am beset on all sides by the peasants with all their petitions full of complaints and these I read rather more unwillingly than my own writings, which I really have no wish to read either."*[100]

Therefore, it is very reasonable that, in the case of his grape buyers as well, Pliny, despite the huge gap between his social status and that of the buyers, had direct knowledge of the buyer's unhappiness with "the deal." This type of personal involvement in the transactional issues with the grape buyers by Pliny brings forward the final business lesson in this chapter dealing with Pliny's business problem.

Lesson 9: Remember Business is Personal

Pliny's personal involvement in his business interests extended well beyond just listening, as he also revealed an acute sensitivity to any perceived unfairness. This is shown very early in his compendium of letters when Pliny requested that an associate of a seller of property intercede to ensure that the buyer, Pliny's close friend Suetonius, obtain a fair (e.g. reduced) price on the purchase of a small property. Pliny went on to say: "A bad bargain is always annoying and especially because it seems to reproach the owner for his folly."[101] The modern expression for this type of situation is *buyer's remorse* and Pliny was cognizant of the impact of the grape merchants' "frustration" and their remorse

Entrepreneurship and Ethics in Ancient Rome

over the deal as priced. Despite the blamelessness of Pliny in this transaction, or perhaps because of it, Pliny could choose to react in any way that he thought necessary to reduce the buyers' remorse for having entered into a situation that became for them a "bad bargain."

The Limits of Pliny's Personal Involvement

If one is seriously looking to establish ongoing business relationships, a cold, arms-length, contractual approach may work fine for major enterprises with their layers of hierarchy and their hierarchy of lawyers but the entrepreneur and small business person does not have that luxury (and perhaps major enterprises should avoid that luxury a bit more frequently). Pliny the gentleman farmer, on the other hand, recognized that his business operations required the personal involvement of the landowner, despite his distinctly superior social status, for he was definitely attuned to his buyers' dashed hopes of a profit on the transaction. We should note, however, that Pliny also cautions that one cannot just respond to complaints, as when he warned a literary correspondent:[102]

> "*experience has shown that appeals for support and sympathy make an immediate strong impact but gradually lose their fire and die down under the influence of reasoned judgment.*"[103]

Since Pliny does respond to the dissatisfaction of his buyers, we can assume he must have thought carefully upon the situation, the seriousness of the financial damage to the buyers and the degree to which he could afford to offer some type of

3 - Pliny's Business Problem

compensation. Pliny did not yield to the terrible sentiment heard far too often today – "It's not personal, it's just business." This powerful and wealthy senator did not insulate himself from the problems of his buyers and dismiss them as he could have done. Instead, Pliny demonstrated that business management is people management and therefore always personal. There must be constant sensitivity to this fact or all parties are diminished in the process.

Chapter Conclusion

In this chapter, we have seen that Pliny's problems are due to the collapse of grape prices causing financial harm to Pliny's grape buyers who purchased Pliny's grape crop in advance of the harvest. Although not contractually obligated to rectify the resultant damage to these merchants, Pliny felt the need to financially assist the buyers and, in so doing, provided us with six additional lessons appropriate to today's business world:

- Lesson 4: Self-Deprecate in Difficult Situations
- Lesson 5: Manage Crises in Person
- Lesson 6: Fully Evaluate Transactional Risks
- Lesson 7: Avoid Single Sourcing
- Lesson 8: Encourage Competition Amongst Partners
- Lesson 9: Remember Business is Personal

Entrepreneurship and Ethics in Ancient Rome

CHAPTER **4**

Pliny's Constraints

We now move from the study of Pliny's business problem to an examination of Pliny's situational constraints. Pliny summarized his assessment of the current pricing situation in the following two sentences:

> "It should have been simple to give them all the same rebate but hardly fair and I hold the view that one of the most important things in life is to practice justice in private as in public life, in small matters as in great and apply it to one's own affairs no less than to other people's. For if we say with the Stoics that 'all offences are equal' the same applies to merits."

Our understanding of the constraints under which Pliny operated begins with his analysis of the viability of issuing a standard rebate to all the grape buyers. We can assume they requested some sort of relief as Pliny informs his readers that it would have been simple just to provide the same rebate to all. We can also infer from the tone of the initial portion of the first sentence above that the practice

Entrepreneurship and Ethics in Ancient Rome

of rebates was not unknown or even unused by Pliny in the past; in this particular instance, however, that traditional practice did not form a constraint for Pliny as he quickly dismissed such an action as "hardly fair." Thus, we have three constraints (traditional practice, expected fairness and same rebate for all) that may have defined a customary rebate sufficient for most grape growers but not for Pliny. The constraints of the customary rebate approach rejected by Pliny can be seen in Figure 4.1 below.

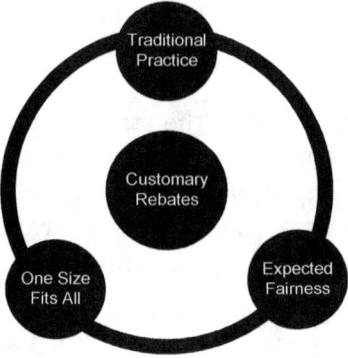

Figure 4.1: Pliny rejected the customary approach to rebates as "hardly fair" in his efforts to create a more expansive and fair program.

Pliny's Efforts to be Fair and Generous

Also, as discussed earlier, we have no clear indication of a contract but even if one existed it would not have constrained Pliny from being more generous than obligated by contract. Despite the inconclusive status of the existence of a contract, we can still assume that Pliny operated under a flexible tradition that demanded no formal obligation on the seller's part to issue rebates for the negative impact of unsettled commodity prices. We can also

4 - Pliny's Constraints

assume that the reverse was certainly true – the buyers would not have remitted a higher price if the market for grapes had dramatically strengthened rather than weakened. Pliny, however, by raising the issue of fairness and also inserting his operating philosophy on justice, unequivocally established for the reader one of the major constraints under which he operated. Pliny, by his own standards, was therefore constrained to be as fair with his buyers as he was in all aspects of his life. A simple and uniform rebate fell short of Pliny's standards for fairness and so he was constrained to do more than what was customary. This desire forms a tactical lesson in Plinian management.

Lesson 10: Be Fair in Business Transactions

We can applaud the goal of fairness in a transaction but we must also remember that fairness is often in the eye of the beholder. In other words, one or more of the recipients of Pliny's program may have seen that which Pliny ultimately perceived as both very generous and fair, as something far less so. Sherwin-White said of the rebate plan that it "sufficed to keep the dealers in business."[104] As we shall see later in the text, the actual size of rebates cannot be precisely ascertained but the point here is that Pliny had no apparent obligation to do anything and was certainly within his rights to don the mantle of fairness for what he did do. Keep in mind that is also why contracts exist, to establish the terms of an agreement that in theory, at least, removes any question of perceived fairness by each party in the beginning of a transaction and not at the end.

Entrepreneurship and Ethics in Ancient Rome

Pliny was perhaps sufficiently influential to simply enforce the deal. That alone could have been argued as enough fairness. Pliny, however, did not do that; instead, he went out of his way to compensate the grape buyers for at least a portion of their losses. Pliny, in his letters, consistently demonstrated that he was a generous man and we can surmise that this was the image he desperately wished to cultivate in this instance, as well. Therefore, it is difficult to gauge which constraint applies here – whether he was generous to the buyers exclusively out of business necessity, or he acted purely for the benefit of his image of generosity. What is more likely was that Pliny acted in a way that satisfied some combination of both constraints.

Regardless of the specific cause for Pliny's actions, the result was the same – he reacted with a generosity that was apparently rare among his fellow Roman senators, for many were far less concerned with their need to be as fair, especially with business partners. For example, Cicero simply dismissed resellers in their entirety as contemptible when he wrote in his book *On Duties* "Vulgar we must consider those who buy from wholesale merchants (such as Pliny's estate) to retail immediately."[105]

4 - Pliny's Constraints

A Counter Example to Pliny's Approach to Business Transactions

A conspicuous instance of the absence of Pliny's sense of fairness can be found in the negotiation practices of Marcus Crassus, a Roman Senator who shared power with Julius Caesar near the end of the Roman Republic. Crassus is believed to have been one of the wealthiest senators in Rome's history with an estimated worth of HS 200 million[106] — ten times that of Pliny. Crassus' approach to fairness in a business transaction also looked a bit different from Pliny's. For, in the crowded city of Rome, Crassus

> "made it his practice to buy houses that were on fire and those in the neighborhood. Which, in the immediate danger and uncertainty the proprietors were willing to part with for little or nothing, so that the greatest part of Rome, at one time or another, came into his hands."[107]

Crassus would probably argue that his method of acquiring property engulfed by flames, or those structures appearing to be threatened, was eminently fair and just. The sellers would have rationally worried that the fire might cause the properties' value to decline even further than Crassus' offer, for if they thought otherwise, they would not have sold. We can debate Crassus' ethical merits of negotiating with a party under such duress but Pliny, based on his actions above, would have been more than skeptical of a claim of fairness if one were to have been put forth by Senator Crassus.

Entrepreneurship and Ethics in Ancient Rome

Figure 4.2: Shows a marble bust of Senator Crassus, one of the wealthiest Senators in ancient Rome's history.[108] Crassus had an estimated wealth that was ten times that of Pliny's.

Pliny's Goal of Fairness

The intention of this lesson, described above as tactical, is to serve as a reminder that, in the process of managing, a plethora of decisions are made daily, both large and small. Each and every one of those decisions, according to Pliny, should be made with an eye to being fair – a tall order but a worthwhile goal for every aspiring business leader.

4 - Pliny's Constraints

Pliny's Standard of Ethics

Pliny fortunately was no Crassus, for after dismissing the simplicity and unfairness of a standard rebate, Pliny told Calvisius Rufus and his entire audience of readers "I hold the view that one of the most important things in life is to practice justice in private as in public life, in small matters as in great and apply it to one's own affairs no less than to other people's." This sentence was more than just a business constraint; it was a summary of one of the core operating principles of Pliny's life. Given the close relationship between Pliny and Calvisius Rufus, Pliny's multiple letters to Calvisius Rufus spanning at least a decade and Pliny elsewhere reminding Calvisius Rufus that, "our close friendship obliges you to act for me as you would yourself",[109] it seems unlikely that Pliny needed to include the above phrasing on private and public justice purely for Calvisius Rufus' benefit. One would have to assume that Pliny included it either for Calvisius Rufus' use, if the letter was to be circulated or read aloud by him, or added it later for the letter's publication to a wider audience. However, that does not diminish the importance of Pliny's stated commitment to justice for our purposes here. Pliny appears to have been intent on demonstrating that the justice of what he was doing in this instance with the grape buyers was simply part of his overall ethical approach to daily life – justice in all public and private business, not just behaving one way for public consumption and another for personal enrichment.

Entrepreneurship and Ethics in Ancient Rome

Pliny the Realist

Pliny, however, was also a realist about the state of ethics in Rome for, in another letter, he laments the contemptible behavior of the majority of his peers when he writes that "very few people are as scrupulously honest in secret as they are in public ... many are influenced by public opinion but scarcely anyone by conscience."[110] Pliny expanded his condemnation of unjust behavior even further when he acknowledged that "I live in a country which has long offered the same (or even greater) rewards to dishonesty and wickedness as it does honor and merit."[111] Despite the temptations, Pliny does not yield and declares "it is not in my nature to do one thing in public and another in private."[112]

Thus we see in Pliny an individual who was obsessed with justice in all that he did, deploring its absence in others and always demanding it from himself. Pliny was so obsessed with acting fairly and being perceived as just that he acknowledged to his readers that "my idea of a truly happy man is one who enjoys the anticipation of a good and lasting reputation."[113] Pliny made it clear that, for him, the ultimate reward — happiness — resulted from living a just life. The gains from doing otherwise may offer material benefit but not a just reputation. This principle of justice formed a central constraint under which Pliny operated. My apologies for the blizzard of Pliny quotes in this section but it is essential to understand that when Pliny was discussing justice, it was not merely for public consumption. If this was simply a case of image making, we would have to assume that with multiple emperors consistently utilizing Pliny's capabilities in the financial arena, one of them would have seen Pliny's self-proclaimed honesty as mere posturing and that was clearly not the case.

4 - Pliny's Constraints

The Emperor Trajan Acknowledges Pliny's Honesty

Trajan himself commented to Pliny in response to a Pliny request for time off to visit his estate: "You have given me many reasons, as well as every official explanation, for your application for leave of absence, though I would have been satisfied with a mere expression of your wishes."[114] Trajan clearly recognized that Pliny was a trustworthy man. Pliny's approach to justice in public and private life brings us to a key lesson in Plinian management that is a strategic complement to the tactical aspect of lesson Ten's requirement to be fair in business transactions.

Lesson 11: Cultivate an Ethical Business Reputation

The modern phrase "Your reputation precedes you" would most likely have been well received not only by Pliny the politician and lawyer but Pliny the businessman. In business today also (and it is in the business sphere that we are focusing) it is inevitable that an enterprise will be seen as an extension of the individuals running it. If a businessperson has a poor reputation so will the business.

The Reputation of Crassus

Returning once more to Senator Crassus, whose questionable practice of purchasing property pushed the boundary of ethical behavior, we see that his actions were certainly in breach of this Plinian constraint. The result of which, as the following two examples show, was that Crassus' reputation more than suffered.

Entrepreneurship and Ethics in Ancient Rome

Our first example deals with the accusation that Crassus attempted to seduce one of Rome's Vestal Virgins. His defense was so sufficiently novel that it was detailed by Plutarch in his biography of Crassus. Plutarch reported that Crassus only admitted that he was attempting to possess her

> "beautiful property in the suburbs ... at a low price, for this reason was frequent in his attentions to her, which gave occasion to the scandal and his avarice, so to say, serving to clear him of the crime, he was acquitted."[115]

Clearly Crassus possessed so great a reputation for avarice that he was even acquitted of attempting to seduce a Vestal Virgin because of it.

The second example related to the reputation of Crassus, recorded by the Roman historian Dio Cassius, shows that Crassus' reputation traveled beyond the borders of Rome and even reached her enemies. Dio reported that upon Crassus' bloody military defeat and death in 53 BC at Carrhae in ancient Syria, a report circulated that the victorious opposing general "poured molten gold into his (Crassus') mouth in mockery (of Crassus' insatiable hunger for riches)."[116] This ignominious end to a talented but selfish leader provides very clear testimony, albeit in the negative, to the importance of Pliny's lesson regarding the need to cultivate an ethical reputation.

4 - Pliny's Constraints

Two Cautions for the Businessperson

We will close this discussion with two necessary cautions with regard to Lesson 11:

1. A businessperson must remember that the technology that so assists in the operation of an enterprise has a dark side as well. That same helpful technology is absolutely unforgiving and unforgetful in its propagation of any ethical lapse if it is memorialized in any electronic fashion. Pliny may never have faced this specific problem but he was exquisitely sensitive to the longevity of his letters and posterity's assessment of their impact on his reputation. One would do well to emulate Pliny's sensitivity to the impact of his actions and words.

2. Operating in a fair and ethical manner does not require individuals to be so generous or trusting in their business dealings as to be constrained to being imprudent. Pliny reminded a rising government official of just that point when he wrote: "trust no one very far. Be always on your guard."[117]

Pliny was ethical but he knew when to be firm. We see that Pliny was certainly no one's fool and any modern executive would be well advised to exercise the same good judgment as Pliny. This lesson on the cultivation of an ethical business reputation should be viewed as the natural result of the cumulative effect of carrying out the requirements of Lesson Ten. The consistent effort to be fair in business transactions is the pedestal upon which one sculpts a reputation for ethical behavior.

Entrepreneurship and Ethics in Ancient Rome

Pliny's Constraints Detailed

We see in the next sentence of Pliny's letter that he recognized he was constrained to begin with the standard approach of equal rebates to all buyers "For if we say with the Stoics that 'all offences are equal' the same applies to merits."

This then reveals that Pliny is thinking that he must establish a uniform baseline rebate for all buyers at a minimum. From Pliny's perspective, he had but few means of realistically salving the pain of the buyers once he decided to do something for them. Other than a rebate, the only other reasonable choice for Pliny would have been to extend the payment terms for the repayment of the buyers' debt. An extension, however, would not have reduced the debt owed to Pliny and would certainly have been less attractive to the buyers since the outstanding debt would only be deferred and would still need to be satisfied in full, ultimately impacting the buyer's cash position. From the buyers' perspective, the rebate approach would appear to have been the best alternative for Pliny to offer.

Pliny Moves Beyond the Customary Rebate Structure

Whatever steps Pliny undertook, his actions had to fit within the constraints of his view of money management – which we have seen was cautious. In addition they had to appear generous but not so generous as to appear indulgent or foolish, impeding his desire for renown. We see from Pliny's perspective that he required a rebate program that moved well beyond the customary rebate structure and constraints as depicted in Figure

4 - Pliny's Constraints

4.1. Instead, Pliny desired a more expansive and complex program that would satisfy the following six constraints:
1. Provide at least a minimum rebate to each buyer.
2. Be just by his personal standards and more fair than was customary.
3. Be sufficiently large as to appear generous but not so large as to appear foolish.
4. Be rationally sized to the sale price of the grapes.
5. Be sufficiently unique to warrant its promotion.
6. Be worth Pliny's investment in time and money.

There was one additional constraint of which Pliny had to be cognizant – the ramifications of any rebate on his future actions. In other words, Pliny needed to be sensitive to the precedence of his actions in this instance. Regardless of Pliny's personal wealth, he was always careful with his capital and any payout above customary amounts could have potentially set a precedent for future harvests that Pliny might be compelled to equal or better. All seven of Pliny's rebate constraints are summarized in Figure 4.3.

We see, despite Pliny's dismissal of a customary approach to a rebate, that he fully understood the need to still operate within the constraints imposed by societal expectations as well as those constraints defined by his exacting personal standards for the

Entrepreneurship and Ethics in Ancient Rome

program. Pliny's sensitivity to these constraints in his design of a rebate program provides us our final management lesson in this chapter.

Lesson 12: Fully Understand your Constraints

Pliny's constraints appear relatively straightforward in retrospect. During a crisis, however, it is often difficult to even define the underlying cause or causes of a problem, let alone the constraints that might bound any solution.

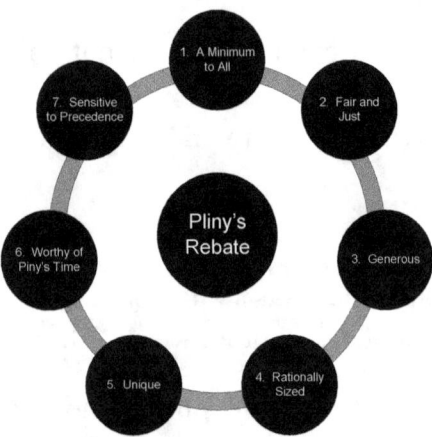

Figure 4.3: Pliny's rebate plan was subject to a combination of both societal and personal constraints, as his program would be subject to public scrutiny and Pliny's own exacting personal standards as well as his expectations for the rebate program's success.

Successful problem resolution requires both cause and constraints to be addressed in concert. If Pliny had merely focused on solving the buyer frustration issue, or the traditional constraints on a grower, he may have chosen a suboptimal solution

4 - Pliny's Constraints

to his problem. Pliny recognized that constraints should be viewed less as limitations and more as boundaries to be understood and used to frame a solution. We often hear of people thinking outside the box to find a solution but to think outside the box one must understand the box and its boundaries or constraints.

A Biblical Example of Overcoming One's Constraints

Whether a business solution is obtained by operating inside or outside one's constraints, the borders should be well understood before they are ignored or accepted as impenetrable. Pliny chose to creatively operate within his constraints. The example that follows, however, is an interesting argument, not only for understanding one's constraints but also the necessity at times to struggle against what appear as impenetrable constraints in order to reach the desired end. In this instance, the constrained businessman was Zacchaeus, an ancient Roman tax collector, whose story is found in the *New Testament*. This is perhaps an ironic choice for a business management text involving Pliny, a persecutor of early Christians in Bithynia (albeit a less than enthusiastic one). The temporal lesson of this biblical parable is relevant to our discussion of constraints. Luke, who was possibly a contemporary of Pliny, wrote of Jesus passing through the town of Jericho, (Luke 19.2-8[118]):

> *"Now a man there named Zacchaeus, who was the chief tax collector and was also a wealthy man, was seeking to see who Jesus was; but he could not see him because of the crowd, for he was short in stature."*

Entrepreneurship and Ethics in Ancient Rome

As a tax collector, especially chief tax collector for the Roman overlords of Judea, Zacchaeus would have been seen as a collaborator, an extortionist and a sinner by his neighbors and, for these reasons, despised by his fellow Jews. Zacchaeus would have well understood that he was truly constrained (and damned) by his reputation. Zacchaeus would have also understood that he was spiritually constrained, as well as physically constrained because of his small size, in his efforts to see Jesus and to obtain any potential forgiveness.

> *"So he ran ahead and climbed up into a sycamore tree in order to see Jesus, who was about to pass that way."*

Zacchaeus determined to overcome his constraints, anticipated the route of Jesus, ran ahead of the crowd and climbed an unclean tree (for its fruit was used to feed pigs and so this further complicated Zacchaeus' efforts to overcome his constraints). Despite this misstep, for no effort is flawless, the tree still allowed Zacchaeus to rise above the crowd (and his physical constraints).

> *"When He reached the place, Jesus looked up and said to him: "Zacchaeus, come down quickly, for today I must stay at your house." And he came down quickly and received him with joy. When they all saw this, they began to grumble, saying: 'He has gone to stay at the house of a sinner.'"*

The elevated Zacchaeus, hated collector of taxes and sinner, is successful in his efforts to be seen by Jesus and is instructed to leave his perch so that Jesus can stay with Zacchaeus. Zacchaeus, however, has one more card to play in his quest for redemption.

4 - Pliny's Constraints

"But Zacchaeus stood there and said to the Lord: 'Behold, half of my possessions, Lord, I shall give to the poor. And if I have extorted anything from anyone, I shall repay it four times over.'"

Zacchaeus has now dealt with his final constraint. The tax-collecting sinner now offers to donate half of his wealth to the poor and even goes a step further. Zacchaeus volunteers to repay fourfold any victims of his extortion in order to achieve the salvation he so desperately seeks. This final action by the unjust Zacchaeus, a disgorgement to his victims of any ill-gotten gains, is an ironically symmetrical plan to the rebate strategy of the just Pliny.

Figure 4.4: Zacchaeus' strategy for overcoming his constraints included the climbing of a tree to catch sight of Jesus. This painting by Niels Larsen Stevns shows Jesus calling Zacchaeus down from his perch.

Entrepreneurship and Ethics in Ancient Rome

The Strategy of Zacchaeus to Overcome his Constraints

As indicated at the beginning of this example, the parable of Zacchaeus is not your typical business case and may appear a bit Sunday schoolish but the lesson of Zacchaeus (see Figure 4.5 below) is both similar and directly relevant to Pliny's situation. To successfully overcome constraints, whether fair or unfair, they must first be understood; second, there must be a determination to leverage all ethical means necessary to facilitate a resolution; third, challenges must be anticipated; and fourth, a comprehensive plan must be developed and implemented.

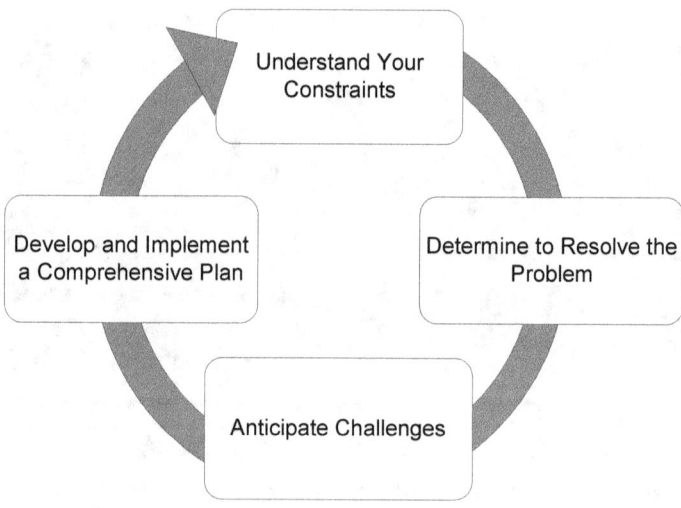

Figure 4.5: The four-step strategy Zacchaeus used in overcoming his constraints.

4 - Pliny's Constraints

Chapter Conclusion

As we close this chapter on Pliny's constraints, we see that we learned three lessons that are applicable to the modern business environment, two of which revolve around the criticality of fairness in business dealings and a third focusing on the need to fully understand one's constraints as part of any problem resolution process:

- Lesson 10: Be Fair in Business Transactions
- Lesson 11: Cultivate an Ethical Business Reputation
- Lesson 12: Fully Understand your Constraints

Entrepreneurship and Ethics in Ancient Rome

CHAPTER 5

Pliny's Solution

Pliny was now at a point in his letter to Calvisius Rufus where he began to define his system of rebates that were subject to the constraints we reviewed in Chapter 4:

> "Accordingly I returned to everyone an eighth of the sum he had spent so that none should depart without a gift of mine."

The baseline rebate to all buyers amounted to one-eighth the size of the agreed upon purchase price. We should ask the question why one-eighth as a rebate was not "fair" as far as Pliny is concerned. Was it not sufficiently fair to mitigate the financial pain felt by the buyers, or was it just too ordinary for Pliny to appear sufficiently generous to his intended audience? From our discussion of constraints in the last chapter, we know that Pliny aimed to be fairer than what may be customary (but not foolishly so). Therefore, it is reasonable to assume that Pliny's baseline rebate of an eighth might normally be considered sufficient but for Pliny, in this case, it

Entrepreneurship and Ethics in Ancient Rome

was not. With the base rebate established at one-eighth, Pliny next revealed his rationale for larger rebates:

> *"Then I made a special provision for those who had invested very large sums in their purchase, since they had been of greater service to me and theirs was the greater loss."*

Purchase Size Mattered to Pliny

In this sentence about "a special provision," Pliny informed his readers that he needed to compensate the buyers who were the larger purchasers of his produce with a larger rebate. His justification for this reasoning was that "they had been of greater service" and "theirs was the greater loss." Pliny's intent to remit back to the grape buyers an additional rebate, calculated based upon purchase size, was certainly rational. Pliny determined that the more significant the buyer in terms of the amount of grapes purchased, the greater the service rendered to him and hence the larger the rebate due. Pliny further defended his decision by stating that the bigger players also had more capital at risk (at least on an absolute basis) than the smaller buyers.

The fact that Pliny had decided to do more for the larger grape buyers than the smaller also indicated that he was very comfortable with the layering of complexity into his rebate calculus in order to accomplish his goal of establishing rebates based upon purchase amounts. This brings us our first lesson of Plinian management in this chapter on the construction of Pliny's solution.

5 - Pliny's Solution

Lesson 13: Ignore Complex Solutions at your own Risk

It is not surprising that Pliny, with significant financial expertise, would be comfortable designing a complex financial solution to the problem at hand. Complexity here had four very real benefits for Pliny:

1. Pliny's complex approach overcame the inherent shortcomings of a "one size fits all" solution by allowing Pliny to customize his rebate plan for different-sized vendors;

2. The complex plan clearly validated Pliny's understanding of the issues at hand;

3. Complex calculations offered additional proof of Pliny's financial competence;

4. The complexly layered approach served as a further demonstration of Pliny's intended generosity to his buyers.

An Additional Example of Pliny's Use of Complex Solutions

This instance with the grape buyers was not the only occasion where Pliny took the time to develop a complex solution to a problem. We see similarly complex elements in Pliny's will (see Appendix F), and we also see his love for complexity in his efforts to assist the poor in his hometown of Comum. In that case, Pliny "promised a capital sum of HS 500,000 for the maintenance of free born boys and girls in the city but, instead of disbursing a lump sum, he transferred property valued greatly in excess of the amount needed to the public land-agent and had it conveyed back to him at a rent of HS 30,000 per annum, thus securing both the principal and the interest for the town."[119]

Pliny's approach to protect his donation from potential abuse by local town officials reinforces the proposition that Pliny was very comfortable choosing the adoption of complex solutions when required (as well as his wisdom in dealing with local officials). This places Pliny at odds with the modern love for brevity and simplicity as summarized in the acronym K.I.S.S. – keep it simple, stupid. The reality is that oversimplification, if it feeds the desire for instant gratification or encourages only a superficial analysis of a problem, can be as detrimental to solution development as unnecessary complexity and the over thinking of an issue.

The point of this lesson is to understand that a complex solution should not be avoided merely because it is complex. It should also be noted that, in order to develop the solution to his problem, Pliny, as any effective manager would, invested the time to fully understand his problem with the harvest and the associated market conditions, as well as the impact of the declining grape prices on the grape buyers. Only after fully analyzing the problem and its constraints did Pliny have the information and confidence needed to devise a solution to the problem at hand.

Pliny's Favoritism

Let's now return to the issue of Pliny's largest buyers. Pliny was certainly more interested in retaining them than the smaller merchants, although he did not ignore the interests of the

5 - *Pliny's Solution*

small — he simply favored the larger players. It has been argued[120] that Pliny's favoritism towards the larger players was actually an effort to retain their good will via quantity discounts. A quantity discount has a similar effect as Pliny's tiered rebate — the reduction of the price paid based upon the quantity purchased — but is typically negotiated at the commencement of a transaction, not at the end. I believe Radice's translation of Pliny here is correct but we should remember that what is most important is not the label but rather Pliny's actions themselves and the results of those actions; in this case, the larger merchants paid less for their grapes than the smaller. Pliny's tilt toward his larger buyers brings us to the second business lesson that emerged from the manner in which Pliny operated with his buyers.

Lesson 14: Incent your Partners

This lesson is intended as a reminder that partnership relations, even those legally formalized, need to be constructed so that there is no ambiguity around the definition of success and that once defined, success can often be best ensured by the careful use of incentives. Examples of performance-based incentives include performance bonuses, volume discounts, improved payment terms and rebates for achievement or overachievement. The measurements of success on which these incentives may be paid include, but are certainly not limited to, speed of delivery (e.g. besting a due date), quantity (e.g. higher production rates), quality (e.g. fewer failures per unit), or volume (e.g. greater amounts purchased). As Pliny demonstrated, it is incumbent upon an outsourcer to establish the appropriate goals and the measurements of those goals as well as the associated incentives to successfully drive the partner behavior to obtain the desired result.

Pliny chose "the Carrot and not the Stick"

Pliny's strategy of utilizing the carrot rather than the stick is really not out of character, given Pliny's emphasis on fairness and generosity. Pliny also articulated his preference for just such an approach when he wrote "affection is far more effective than fear in gaining your ends."[121] As we have seen above, Pliny followed his own advice when it came to dealing with his grape buyers for he bought their "affection" with extra sesterces and, as mentioned earlier, there was no sign of using his powerful social position or wealth as a stick to engender fear in his partners. This approach to dealing with his partners would most likely not have sat well with Pliny's hero, Cicero. Cicero not only disdained "vulgar" resellers, but also he declared "they would get no profits without a great deal of downright lying."[122] With respect to Pliny's grape merchants then, it would appear that Cicero's views had much more in common with those of Petronius rather than Pliny, who intuited that his resellers, despite the need for an occasional incentive to help ensure the proper results, were not to be disparaged or threatened but rather were to be valued and retained.

Do not Forget the "Stick"

This discussion of incentives would not be complete if we did not mention the applicability of "fear" in a partner relationship. Pliny stated that affection

5 - Pliny's Solution

is more effective than fear but he did not say that fear is ineffective. In a partnership relationship, fear can also be contracted through the establishment of performance penalties, often based on the same criteria as the incentives. The traditional downside of penalties is that they work well in the short term but tend to work against the formation of a long-term relationship. This is because penalties, when assessed, are indicative of a partnership that is failing to meet the contracted measures of success and often better serve as a clarion call for one or both parties to rethink the benefit of continuing such a relationship or at least to re-evaluate the structure of the relationship. That said, the appropriate blending of both performance incentives and penalties in a contract remain an effective tool in driving partner performance.

Pliny Defines Large

Pliny next defined what he meant by the "large" amounts invested by the more significant buyers and informed Calvisius Rufus what he intended for those buyers he considered to be of "greater service." It should be noted that Pliny first described the one-eighth rebate as a "special grant" (see below). This validates the point that the rebate was clearly not a legal obligation for Pliny. This reference makes it very clear that Pliny considered the rebate a gift that he gave the buyers (which of course reinforced his reputation for generosity and his partners' obligations to him in the future). The sentence reads:

> "I therefore allowed everyone whose purchases had cost him more than 10,000 sesterces a tenth of anything he had spent above the 10,000, in addition to the original eighth which was sort of a special grant."

Despite Pliny's great wealth, we see that Pliny considered a buyer committing over HS 10,000 "large" and subject to special attention. This is somewhat surprising, given the earlier example of Pliny the Elder's involving the purchase of HS 400,000 worth of grapes on the vine. It is a bit difficult to reconcile a range of "large transactions" that spans HS 10,000 to HS 400,000. Nonetheless, Pliny felt merchants purchasing at least HS 10,000 of grapes from his estate were sufficiently large and warranted special treatment. This is not the only time we see Pliny extremely concerned with amounts of capital that might first appear as relatively small amounts of money to a man of his wealth. As a financial appointee of the Emperor Trajan, Pliny wrote to the Emperor:

> "I was informed that a delegate was sent annually to offer you a loyal address and allow(ed) 12,000 sesterces for his expenses ... I decided to send on the address but no delegate to convey it, so the citizens could reduce expenses without failing in their official duty towards you."[123]

Clearly, Pliny was a man that closely monitored the public finances of the emperor, both large and small, as carefully as he managed his personal finances. (It should be noted that Pliny's superior, the Emperor Trajan, wrote back to Pliny that he was pleased with the HS 12,000 savings.) To put the

5 - Pliny's Solution

level of financial detail here that concerned Pliny into another perspective, we need to understand that this is the same man who told a childhood friend[124] "your present capital is 100,000 sesterces, so I want to give you another 300,000 to make up your qualification for the (equestrian) order."[125] Pliny may have possessed great wealth and may have been exceedingly generous to his friends but he was also simultaneously meticulous in the control he exercised managing financial expenditures, public or private. This approach of Pliny's financial management establishes our initial Plinian lesson on cash management.

Lesson 15: Micromanage your Capital

This lesson is not an argument against aggressive investment or for the strangulation of growth but rather a caution that a firm's capital needs to be managed closely and processes established to monitor all expenses, both major and minor in size. Pliny's technique of viewing all expenditures (no matter how small) as significant may not be novel to the modern CFO but in a business organization it is also imperative that all leaders — not just the financial staff — emulate Pliny's careful approach to money management. Additionally, entrepreneurs and executives alike should demonstrate their care for their business' finances by conducting audits (on both a scheduled and an unscheduled basis) of the company's dispersal of funds to ensure funds are utilized as intended. This approach serves as a clear reminder to employees that all expenditures, regardless of their size, are in fact closely monitored and important.

Entrepreneurship and Ethics in Ancient Rome

Pliny's Discipline

Pliny again demonstrated the need to be disciplined in the management of capital in another of his many letters to Tacitus. This particular piece of correspondence discussed the education of the young in Pliny's hometown and detailed the methods he utilized for making a donation to his hometown to fund the hiring of teachers. Pliny informed Tacitus that he would have considered paying the entire amount required by the town but was concerned that, if he did so, his gift might be squandered if the parents had no financial participation in the funding of the program as he had seen elsewhere when teachers were compensated by the government.

Pliny was clearly well versed in the problem of waste in publicly-funded programs, the potential for the abuse of private grants and the curse of nepotism by public officials[126]. Therefore, Pliny only offered to match the parents' contribution on a two to one basis (1/3 of the cost) and in this same letter, Pliny informed Tacitus of his rationale:

> "People who may be careless about another person's money are sure to be careful about their own and they will see that only a suitable recipient shall be found for my money if he is also to have their own."[127]

We continue to see that Pliny was consistently careful in the management of his capital and its application. Pliny worked diligently to ensure that each and every sesterce utilized was accounted for and produced the result he desired. Just as he did with the grape buyers' rebate, Pliny designed the structure of his educational donation to ensure

5 - Pliny's Solution

that it was no simple giveaway. To accomplish this, Pliny created what we would call today a charitable matching program where a single donor matches the contributions of others, usually up to a certain amount and in a specified ratio.

Today's Need for Disciplined Capital Management

This insight into the necessity of careful financial management is as relevant to the modern business world as it was in Pliny's day. All employees (not just the company's leadership team) must be a vigilant in protecting company assets. A key means of accomplishing this goal is to ensure that employee compensation is tightly aligned to the company's money management goals just as Pliny used his funds to tie parents into the hiring of quality instructors for the their children (and, as we will see later, used the grape buyer rebate to drive certain behavior as well).

Conversely, a businessperson's inattentiveness to the control of company assets can quickly lead to financial ruin, as again vividly expressed by Petronius. Returning to the bankrupt undertaker forced to auction his furniture because of financial reversals, Petronius detailed the real cause of Julius Proculus' misfortune: "his crooked friends stripped him to feather their own nests."[128] Proculus, unlike Pliny, failed to carefully judge his friends or manage his capital and was quickly separated from it. We see the old saying that "a fool and his money are soon parted" may have applied to Gaius Julius Proculus but not to Pliny. In today's economy, we also have another important saying – "cash is king" – and that adage is one that Pliny would have eagerly embraced, as demonstrated by his micromanagement of his capital. The importance of cash and its management to a business remains as critical today as it was in Pliny's day.

Calculating Pliny's Rebates

Pliny next proceeds to do a sample calculation for Calvisius Rufus in order to fully illustrate the steps involved in determining the rebate for larger players and calculating the amount of capital Pliny would ultimately be returning to the buyers.

> "I am afraid I have put it badly; let me try to make my calculations clearer. Suppose someone had offered the sum of 15,000 sesterces; he would receive an eighth of 15,000 plus a tenth of 5,000."

As mentioned earlier, it is difficult to know if the sample calculation given in this letter was in the original to Calvisius Rufus or added by Pliny for the book's publication. The inclusion of an example in this letter by Pliny is in no way unique (see Carlon pages 182-183) and, as Carlon notes; Pliny uses examples in 58 of the letters contained in his first nine books. The rebate scheme was very complex and Pliny clearly understood that the best means of ensuring clarity was not only to explain in detail each step of the computation but to offer his readers a sample calculation also. Pliny's intent with the provision of a sample calculation establishes a lesson that Pliny has applied to both his oral and written communications.

5 - Pliny's Solution

Lesson 16: Know your Audience

Pliny spent years arguing in the courts and was considered one of the great orators of his day. Pliny was, therefore, aware of the need to ensure that his message was well prepared and the artful presentation of his arguments typically required a significant investment of his time. In a lengthy letter to Tacitus discussing oratory, Pliny states that brevity "is desirable ... but if it means that points which should be made are omitted, or hurried over when they should be impressed and driven home by repetition, one can only end by betraying one's client."[129] Pliny appears to have approached the use of his words exactly as he did with the use of his capital: with forethought and precision, as well as a studied understanding of the recipients.

Pliny desired to be as clear as possible for the potential audience of Letter 8.2 and repeated himself via a detailed example to ensure that there was no confusion in his communication of the mechanics used to calculate the rebate amounts to an audience that Pliny anticipated would lack his financial sophistication. Like Pliny, a modern entrepreneur must strive to understand his or her audience (examples might include customers, employees, bankers and investors), or the resulting ignorance may have very serious consequences for one's business interests, such as the loss of investor confidence, employee morale, or customers. It is essential, therefore, to gain as comprehensive an understanding of a message's audience as is feasible and to accommodate the strengths and weaknesses of the chosen medium of communication.

Entrepreneurship and Ethics in Ancient Rome

In today's age of powerful search engines, computational technology, huge databases and instant communication, the ability to understand one's audience has moved from an ancient art form to a science. As a result, the opportunity to misread one's audience should be dramatically reduced. However, significant management involvement is still required in order to avoid the age-old pitfall of missing the mark and it must remembered that without the experienced guidance of the responsible executive, the mere application of staff, sophisticated technology and money will guarantee nothing.

Additionally, as the potential size of one's audience shrinks from those external to one's business organization to those within, the technological tools available for gaining insights into the audience diminish and can be further restricted by company policy or statute. Regardless of the tools, there is no substitute for the institutional knowledge that is gained over time through an executive's consistent interaction with employees and coworkers. Finally, the smallest audiences require the greatest familiarity but offer the fewest automated tools to assist in the effort.

An Ancient Example of Misreading an Audience

An extreme example of the penalty for misreading an audience can again be found in Petronius' *Satyricon*, which contains an interesting story of an entrepreneurial glassmaker and his once-in-a lifetime audience with the Emperor Tiberius.

5 - Pliny's Solution

Figure 5.1: A marble bust of a young Tiberius[130] whom Pliny the Elder called the "most gloomy of men."[131] Following the death of the Emperor Augustus, Tiberius became Emperor in 14 AD (he was in his mid-fifties) and reigned until his death in 37 AD.

Tiberius is certainly better known for his employment of Pontius Pilate as his governor of Judea rather than for this incident; however, the events described by Petronius fit well within both Tacitus' and Suetonius' characterization of Tiberius.

Entrepreneurship and Ethics in Ancient Rome

The Tale of the Glassmaker

Petronius wrote:

> "there once was a workman who invented a little glass bottle that wouldn't break. Well, he got in to see the emperor with this bottle as a present. Then he asked the emperor to hand it back to him and managed to drop it on the floor on purpose. Well, the emperor just about died. But the workman picked the bottle up from the floor and, believe it or not, it was dented just a little, as though it were made out of bronze. So he pulled a little hammer out of his pocket and tapped it back into shape. Well, by this time he thought he had Jupiter by the balls, especially when the emperor asked him if anyone else was in on the secret. But you know what happened? When the workman told him that nobody else knew, the emperor ordered his head chopped off. Said that if the secret ever got out, gold would be cheap as dirt."[132]

Though a less dramatic version of this story can also be found in Pliny's uncle's *Natural History*,[133] both versions share one critical component – the consequences of a failure to understand one's audience.

Pliny was Always Prepared

Pliny, a survivor of many emperors and, according to his own letters, seemingly always prepared, would never make the novice's mistake of misreading his audience, especially an emperor. Based on his extensive experience, he even shared with his readers his thoughts on how to be prepared to instruct an emperor without appearing to overstep the boundaries of propriety. He wrote:

5 - Pliny's Solution

"To proffer advice on an Emperor's duties might be a noble enterprise but it would be a heavy responsibility verging on insolence, whereas to praise an excellent ruler and thereby shine a beacon on the path posterity should follow would be equally effective without appearing presumptuous."[134]

Pliny's was always exquisitely prepared for any endeavor and perhaps spontaneity was not Pliny's strong suit but his model still stands in good stead for any businessperson embarking on a meeting with a superior: there is absolutely no substitute for thorough preparation and the even the slightest appearance of arrogance should be avoided at all costs.

Pliny's Rebate as a Management Tool

At this point in Pliny's letter, we see just how far he was taking the concept of the rebate. Pliny had already recognized the damage from the collapse of grape prices and the size of the commitment made by each of his buyers. Now Pliny, in the two sentences that follow, went on to say he felt the need to recognize the fact that some of his buyers paid down significant portions of what they owed him prior to receiving and reselling the harvest:

> *"Moreover, in view of the fact that some people had paid down large installments of what they owed, while others had paid little or nothing, I thought it most unfair to treat them all with the same generosity in granting a rebate when they had not been equally conscientious in discharging their debts. Once more, then, I allowed another tenth of the sum received to those who paid."*

Entrepreneurship and Ethics in Ancient Rome

Pliny returned one-tenth of the "sum received" from any cash that had been prepaid by a buyer. In this final element of his complex rebate system, Pliny was acknowledging that any capital already received from a buyer was another very important element of their business relationship that must be recognized and rewarded via an additional rebate.[135]

Pliny the Micromanager

Pliny, by deciding to recognize the buyers that had already paid a portion of their debts to him, also revealed how extremely close he was to the financial transactions at hand. He was fully conversant in the accounts receivables from each purchaser, because he was rewarding the conscientiousness of the buyers who were proactive in settling some or all of their outstanding debt to Pliny. Given Pliny's penchant for financial analysis, it is no surprise that he also stayed close to the debts owed to the estate and potentially knew the receivables due from each individual buyer associated with the purchase of his grape harvest. This establishes a second Plinian lesson in capital management. Lesson 15 dealt with the care required for managing one's capital and the following lesson further extends that concept with the conscientious handling of one's debtors.

Lesson 17: Closely Monitor Receivables

Pliny's detailed knowledge of his receivables further strengthens the case for just how intimately involved Pliny was in the management of his estates. As we have seen before, Pliny was nothing if not consistent and so, in another of his letters relating to his agribusiness, Pliny again demonstrated a keen

5 - Pliny's Solution

awareness of the debts owed him, this time by his tenant farmers and the importance of dealing with that debt. In Pliny's correspondence with a friend recently elevated to the consulship, Pliny apologizes for needing to miss the inauguration ceremony:

> *"I love you too much to fear you will misinterpret my intentions if I am not present when you take up the consulship on the first of the month; especially when I must stay here... During the past five years, despite the large reductions I have made in rents, the arrears have increased."*[136]

Again we see a man who was on site personally handling a problem, the importance he placed on the resolution of his tenants' debts (he would not leave for Rome to attend his friend's important inaugural event) and his familiarity with his tenants' financial problems.

Modern Cash Management

Pliny was consistently focused on his capital and the importance of collecting receivables to ensure the ongoing preservation of his cash. All businesses generate accounts receivable and the rate at which they collect what is due (e.g. days' sales outstanding) is a key business measurement for determining the stability of a business, as is the size of a company's bad debt reserve for uncollectable debts. The successful entrepreneur must be as cognizant of these measurement criteria as those implemented for tracking revenue and the sales pipeline. These measures assist in the management of a company's cash position and the failure to closely monitor the collection of cash is a critical shortcoming, for a company's revenue is not tangible until the cash is in hand. Pliny was as unfailingly attentive to the importance of cash collections as he was to cash disbursements.

Pliny the Creditor

One final point on the debts owed to Pliny needs to be made. The inverse of the debt relationship of the tenant farmers and the grape buyers to Pliny was the fact that Pliny extended credit to both sets of parties. History has unfortunately shown the extension of credit to tenant farmers typically resulted in their seemingly perpetual debt to their landlords with the result that by "the end of the third century, tenants were tied (to the farm), not free."[137] So despite Pliny's good nature and generosity, this type of debt bondage for the tenant farmers was similar to and foreshadowed the later emergence of serfdom in the middle ages.

Alternatively, Pliny's credit extension to grape buyers appeared to have no negative long-term effect on these small businessmen, which would seem to indicate that the business model for the buyers was in fact sufficiently profitable so that debts could generally be repaid after the harvest. Perhaps the repayments were not always done with the consistency that Pliny might have liked (as seen by his efforts to accelerate debt repayments via the rebate) but given the long-term relationships and Pliny's comments regarding the buyers' conscientiousness, in this case the model worked for the benefit of the creditor and debtor alike.

5 - Pliny's Solution

Pliny's "Gratitude" Towards his Buyers

In revealing his appreciation for those who paid down their debt, Pliny informed us of the two reasons for his actions. Let us therefore parse the sentence into its two segments and analyze each separately:

> *"This seemed a suitable way both of expressing my gratitude to each individual according to his past merits* and of encouraging them all not only to buy from me in the future but also to pay their debts."

Pliny first informed Calvisius Rufus that he was actually demonstrating his "gratitude" for "past merits." Since Pliny linked gratitude with past merits in this sentence and he is nothing if not precise, then we must conclude that individual buyers had long-term relationships through multiple harvests with Pliny and he valued those relationships. This allows us to further assume that Pliny likely preferred not to find and negotiate with a new set of grape buyers annually. If Petronius was accurate in his description of the grape merchants, we can understand why Pliny would not want to initiate a buyer selection process with undue frequency and also to incur the challenge of breaking in the new buyers prior to each harvest season. After all, the price negotiation with his existing partners alone must have been a rather time consuming effort even without the complication of beginning a new relationship.

We can also infer that by Pliny's reference to "past merits," he was referring to buyers who performed well from Pliny's perspective.

Entrepreneurship and Ethics in Ancient Rome

Performance here might have meant that Pliny's buyers historically operated effectively at harvest time to complete their end of the agreement and as importantly, debt due to Pliny was paid as required. Pliny's recognition of the value of long-term relationships with his buyers provides our second lesson on the management of partner relationships and the final lesson for this chapter.

Lesson 18: Build Long-term Partner Relationships

There are very practical benefits that accrue from the establishment of a long-term relationship with a partner. One key benefit is the degree of intimacy and familiarity that is generally not immediately possible with new business partners and that allows both parties to comfortably and quickly react to unexpected challenges in tandem, avoiding the difficulties that can often occur during the early stages of any relationship. Considering Pliny's elevated social status, his public responsibilities and his multiplicity of estates, it would appear that any personal contact and relationship development with buyers would be gradual, perhaps having required a period of years to mature. Given both Pliny's penchant for direct involvement and his knowledge of the buyers' frustration, we can assume just such a relationship did in fact form, however, so Pliny was able to react to the collapse in grape prices with the confidence that came from having established a solid working relationship with his estate's long-term partners.

A second benefit of a long-term relationship is that, once established, the initial and often

5 - Pliny's Solution

lengthy process of formalizing the relationship can be avoided during the balance of the engagement. For Pliny, the annual process of selling the grape harvest would have been greatly simplified because all parties should have known the routine and this too might help to explain the absence of any reference to a contract. Today, many businesses attempt to avoid the challenge and costs of rebidding contracts annually by extending out contract terms for multiple years, often with the inclusion of renewal options that simply require the approval of the outsourcing partner or that renew if one or both parties fail to cancel by a certain date; however, care must still be taken (e.g. via audits and pricing comparisons) to ensure that a long-term relationship does not become counter productive from a competitive bid perspective.

Pliny and His Market

Pliny appeared fully committed to the benefits of a long-term relationship with his buyers, although he worked to ensure that they did not live on "past merits" by "encouraging" them to continue to perform going forward:

> "This seemed a suitable way both of expressing my gratitude to each individual according to his past merits **and of encouraging them all not only to buy from me in the future but also to pay their debts.**"

Pliny was forthright in his intentions when he stated that a goal of this rebate was to encourage the buyers to do business with him and his estate in the future. Since Pliny did not utilize any other means to sell his grape production, Pliny relied solely on his buyers and recognized that these resellers were in fact his market for the grapes produced on his estate. Pliny clearly wanted to keep this market intact for the long-term and, in order to guarantee that future harvests had reliable buyers, he was willing to reduce their business risks with his cash as the means of encouragement.

A second justification that Pliny provided for the financial incentive is also detailed. Pliny wanted to encourage his resellers to "pay their debts"— again emphasizing Pliny's fixation on capital management but also indicating that historical performance of the buyers may not have always included 100% debt repayment to Pliny or repayment at the time required. Pliny desired to reduce the future risk that they would fail to pay for forthcoming harvests and was willing to incentivize his buyers in an effort to minimize that risk.

Pliny was clearly looking past his immediate problems and realized that in order to reduce future uncertainty he needed financially stable business partners. Pliny would have known that he could not affect future grape prices but he could strengthen the financial well being of his partners and also encourage them to reduce their debts to him. Not all problems lend themselves to such a forward-looking solution but whenever a situational analysis is being conducted, the problem being confronted should ideally be examined as Pliny demonstrated — from the perspective of past experiences, present conditions and future considerations, if possible (and not unduly constrained by time).

5 - Pliny's Solution

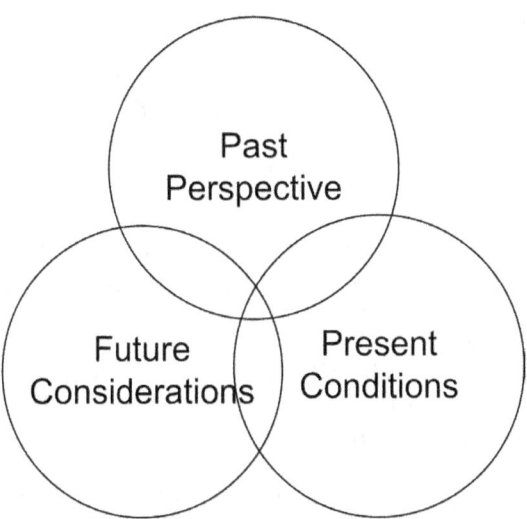

Figure 5.2: Shows time frames impacting any situational analysis. An examination of one's problem from each of these perspectives can be very helpful when framing a solution.

Balancing Partner Competition with Long-term Relationships.

We should also note that, despite the recognized benefits of long-term relationships, many of today's companies are so driven by cost containment that they look to change partners as often as one might change one's clothing. This is obviously a means of improving the short-term profits as we discussed in Lesson 8 when we reviewed the need for partner competition; however, when this competitive model is pushed too far, relationships fail to form and the benefits of long-term relationships at best are diminished and possibly completely lost. Lessons 8 and 18 need not be mutually exclusive but they do require there be appropriate consideration of both and a balanced implementation of each.

Entrepreneurship and Ethics in Ancient Rome

Chapter Conclusion

In this chapter, we saw the final construction of Pliny's solution, a complex rebate addressing four needs of Pliny's:

1. To salve the short term frustration of his grape buyers due to the collapse of grape prices;
2. To pay an incentive for the grape buyers conducting large amounts of business with Pliny's estate;
3. To reward the grape buyers that maintained a long term business relationship (loyalty) with Pliny's estate; and
4. To offer an incentive for the entire set of grape buyers to pay down their debt to Pliny as quickly as possible.

From Pliny's construction of a rebate program that met these needs (and successfully navigated his complex set of operating constraints) we were able to establish six management lessons:

- Lesson 13: Ignore Complex Solutions at your own Risk
- Lesson 14: Incentivize your Partners
- Lesson 15: Micromanage your Capital
- Lesson 16: Know your Audience
- Lesson 17: Closely Monitor Receivables
- Lesson 18: Build Long-term Buyer Relationships

CHAPTER 6

Pliny's Outcome

Pliny transformed a difficult situation on his Tuscan estate into an opportunity to assist his grape buyers and to help ensure the stability of the estate's future business. He was satisfied with the results of his rebate program and he gloated to Calvisius Rufus in the closing portion of his letter:

> "My system – or my good nature – has cost me a lot but it has been worth it."

Pliny was sufficiently pleased with himself over the success of the program to intentionally contravene one of his own tenets regarding self-aggrandizement expressed in a very early letter when Pliny wrote that good deeds must not be exposed and "in fact it is only when good deeds are consigned to obscurity and silence that they escape criticism and misconstruction."[138] Pliny, in this instance, must have decided, after his return to Rome, that the rebate's results were just too good to "consign to obscurity" and so he chose to widely promote his actions and risk "criticism and misconstruction."

Entrepreneurship and Ethics in Ancient Rome

Pliny clearly rationalized that the benefits that accrued from his self-promotion in this case outweighed the associated risks.

Next, Pliny gently joked about his "good nature" costing him "a lot" in a manner similar to his opening sentence in this letter; however, Pliny was now very explicit as to why he returned from his estate poorer – because of the cost of his rebate system and his good-natured generosity. Looking back over nearly 2,000 years, "a lot" is rather difficult to measure but it is important at this point to attempt the effort and to try to size the actual cost of the rebate system that Pliny is so willing to describe as leaving him the poorer for it. We know Pliny was careful with his money and that his complaints of estate losses have on occasion appeared exaggerated. In one letter to a relative, the wealthy Pliny goes so far as to say that his income "deficiencies can be made up by simple living."[139]

Estimating the Financial Impact of Pliny's Rebates

The question is whether Pliny's complaints about the rebate program's cost are another exaggeration or were they warranted? With respect to the cost of the rebate we must remember that the rebate was a percentage of the total amount owed by each buyer to Pliny and that the total any one buyer owed Pliny would have included Pliny's profit on the sale of the grape harvest as well. Although we do not know Pliny's profit margin on the sale of the grapes, we can establish a plausible range. Using a letter[140] by Pliny to the Emperor Trajan requesting the authority to lower his province's official short-term

6 - Pliny's Outcome

interest rate down from 12% to 6%, we can assume that if Pliny chose to place his capital in agriculture, his return should have exceeded the short term cost of money. Therefore, we can conclude that 12% was the expected minimum return (the floor) on the sale of the grapes. To assist us in the determination of Pliny's maximum potential profit margin, we must turn to a modern review of an ancient source. The retired soldier and farmer Lucius Junius Moderatus Columella wrote the most detailed source we have on Roman agriculture in the first century AD. M. I. Finley, in *The Ancient Economy*, called his ancient farming text *De Re Rustica* "the most reliable ancient analysis of Italian farm income."[141] However, Finley then went on to trash the associated financial analysis: "His (Columella) implied 34% annual return is nonsense."[142] Thus, we can infer that, if Finley were correct, Pliny's maximum profit should not have exceeded 34% (the ceiling). We now have possible limits for Pliny's return on the sale of his grapes – a profit margin somewhere between 12% and 34%.

Although we do not know the number of buyers used by Pliny, it is not difficult to estimate the percentage range of the rebates granted by Pliny since he was very precise in his letter to Calvisius Rufus. Pliny stated that all the buyers received a minimum of one-eighth of their purchase back (Step 1). Those with a transaction larger than 10,000 sesterces received an additional 10% of the amount over HS 10,000 (Step 2). Finally those who paid down some portion of their debt to Pliny in advance of the harvest were rebated an additional 10% of what was paid in (Step 3). So, let us next perform a few calculations based on Pliny's rebate model to

Entrepreneurship and Ethics in Ancient Rome

determine how the financial impact of the rebates fits within the theoretical bounds on profit that we just established.

Calculating Pliny's Minimum Rebate

First, the minimum rebate would occur if a buyer purchased HS 10,000 or less of the grapes and did not prepay any of his debt to Pliny. Therefore, the minimum rebate a buyer would be entitled to was 12.5% as seen in the steps below:

Step 1: One-eighth of the total purchased by a buyer: 12.5%

Step 2: Add 10% of the purchase amount over 10,000: 0%

Step 3: Add 10% of the purchase amount prepaid: 0%

Minimum Total: 12.5% of the Purchase Amount

Calculating the Theoretical Maximum Rebate

To obtain the maximum rebate we would need to know the purchases over HS 10,000 made by the buyers as well as the amount they each prepaid. We do not know either but we can establish a theoretical upper limit by allocating a 10% rebate for Step 2 which can never be reached since Pliny only granted an additional 10% only on the amounts over HS 10,000 (not on the total purchase) and also by allocating a maximum of 10% for Step 3 (the most a buyer could have earned by prepaying the entire amount owed Pliny). Therefore, the maximum rebate

6 - Pliny's Outcome

a buyer would be entitled to must have been less than 32.5% as seen in the steps below:

Step 1: One-eighth of the total purchased by a buyer: 12.5%

Step 2: Add additional 10% of the total purchase: 10%

Step 3: Add 10% of entire purchase for complete prepayment: 10%

Theoretical Maximum Total: 32.5% of the Purchase Amount

Calculating Pliny's Sample Rebate

One last calculation should be done to establish a sample rebate between the minimum and the theoretical maximum. For our purposes here, let's choose HS 15,000 as the purchase size of a buyer since Pliny's used HS 15,000 for his calculation (Sherwin-White estimated[143] that HS 15,000 was in fact the maximum unit of sale for each grape buyer). If we also assume that this theoretical buyer prepaid half (HS 7,500) of the entire purchase amount, the buyer would have received a rebate of 20.8% as seen in the steps below:

Step 1: One-eighth of the total of HS 15,000: HS 1,875

Step 2: Add 10% of the amount (HS 5,000) over HS 10,000: HS 500

Step 3: Add 10% of amount (HS 7,500) prepaid: HS 750

Sample Buyer Total: HS 3,125 (20.8% of the Purchase Amount)

We have now seen that Pliny never rebated amounts less than 12.5% or more than 32.5%. From the sample calculation, 20.8% of the purchase price would have been rebated by Pliny and as little as 15.8% if there were no prepayment (an amount Sherwin-White felt offered survivability to the buyers). We should also note that, if the entire amount of HS 15,000 had been prepaid, Pliny would still have only rebated an additional HS 750 for a total rebate to the buyer of 25.8% of the purchase price.

From our earlier discussion of the potential profit margin on Pliny's sale of his grape harvest, we should note that Pliny appears to have established his minimum rebate (12.5%) very close to our theoretical lower limit of 12% profit on the sale of his grapes and a maximum rebate (32.5%) bounded by the 34% upper limit. Despite Finley's distrust of Columella's profit estimate, it is very interesting to find that Pliny's maximum theoretical rebate is less than the 34% postulated by Columella. This can be readily seen in Figure 7.1 below comparing Pliny's rebates at varying prepayment percentages.

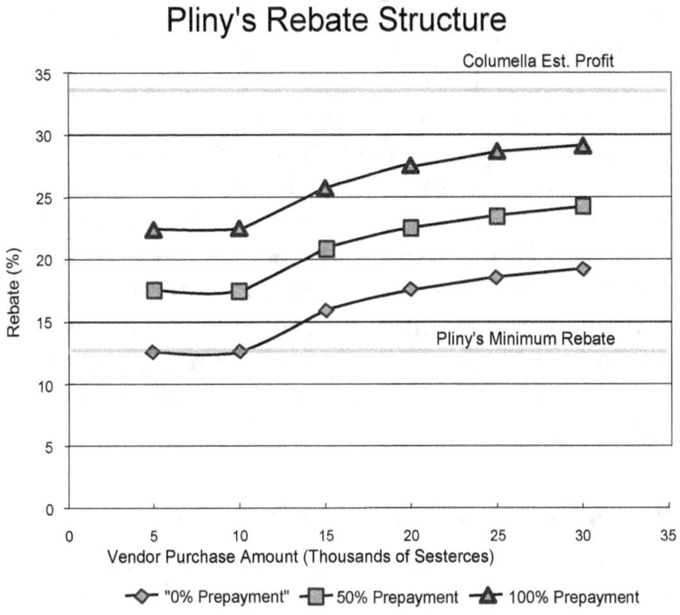

6 - Pliny's Outcome

Pliny's Rebate Structure

Figure 6.1: A plot of Pliny's rebates for varying prepayment percentages showing the rebates bounded by Pliny's commitment for a guaranteed minimum payment and Columella's profit estimate for ancient Italian farm income.

Pliny's Rebates between 12.5% and 32.5%

Although Columella died while Pliny was still a child, it would not be surprising if Pliny had been familiar with Columella's work and that Columella's estimated return possibly served as a critical benchmark for Pliny that he was determined not to exceed. Alternatively, Pliny may simply have based his figures on his own historical returns. Regardless of the source of Pliny's constraints on the amounts to be rebated, and despite Pliny's complaints about the rebate program's cost, he most likely did not rebate more than his anticipated profit margin on the sale of his grape harvest and would have retained from each vendor between 67.5% and 87.5% of the original bid. We know that Pliny could afford the rebate since he voluntarily chose to implement the plan but we must remember that he was still returning at least a minimum of an eighth (12.5% of the purchase price) to every buyer. Any business today refunding anywhere near this amount of its annual revenue would, like Pliny, also say the program was costing "a lot" and that they were very much "the poorer for it." It is also doubtful that members of a modern company's management team would be joking about their good nature in doing so (even if they were still employed).

Pliny's Rebates Costly but "worth it"

We now have sized the rebate program and perhaps even defined "a lot" as seen through Pliny's eyes (and "survivability" in Sherwin-White's). We should also note that if Pliny did not feel that his rebate were truly significant there really would be no need for this letter. The risk of embarrassment would far outweigh any benefit. Conversely, whether Pliny was the poorer for it has to be judged on two levels – the first is the rebate program itself, which did cost Pliny some (if not all) of his anticipated profit on the season's grape crop. The second is the loss of income relative to Pliny's wealth and, on this level too, it is difficult to argue that the rebates truly left Pliny the poorer for it.

Regardless of the rebates' impact on Pliny's wealth, we do know that with the rebate, which was significant to the grape buyers' financial well being, Pliny was attempting to obtain specific short-term benefits as well as induce appropriate long-term

6 - Pliny's Outcome

financial behavior from his buyers. Given Pliny was attempting to address a short term problem as well as drive longer term performance, the rebate program's cost was more than just an expense; it evolved into an investment in the estate's future. This investment by Pliny establishes another management lesson from Pliny.

Lesson 19: Delineate Investment Objectives

There was no ambiguity about Pliny's investment objectives. The money paid to the buyers was intended to encourage future purchases and debt repayment as well as to purchase loyalty toward Pliny's estate. Pliny's investments in his buyers were well thought out and fully aligned with both his short and long-term needs. If he had merely returned an equal percentage of each buyer's purchase he would have possibly reduced frustration but brought no longer-term value to his interests. We saw the same approach in the educational donations discussed earlier. Pliny, in that instance, was using his money to encourage long-term meritorious behavior by the citizens of his district, eliminating nepotism and keeping the townsfolk involved in the process of educating their children.

Modern Implications from Pliny's Lesson

Today, we see legions of accountants working to ensure that the Return on Investment (ROI) of any investment is properly measured and analyzed. Such work is essential to any investment decision but not directly relevant to our lesson here. Financial reports must always be examined but what we

Entrepreneurship and Ethics in Ancient Rome

learn from Pliny is that it is also necessary to reach beyond the numbers to understand the operational implications of any business investment. It is the benefits from a business investment that drive finances and not the reverse. Far too often, managers overanalyze "the numbers" and use them as a surrogate for the time required to gain an understanding of the underlying strengths and weaknesses of a business opportunity. We should also remember that Pliny's love affair with complex financial elements was not simply an end in itself or a mere public relations ploy but rather his particular approach to ensuring that operational objectives were delineated and that his investments were properly aligned with those objectives. Last, given Pliny's careful attention to money management, he would never have been cavalier with any expenditure unless he felt the achievement of his goals was worth the cost.

In fact, Pliny may have been well aware of a favorite saying of the Emperor Augustus, documented by his friend Suetonius and very much in line with Pliny's cautious approach to his business dealings. The Emperor Augustus often advised his commanders not to fish "with a golden hook, the loss of which, if it were carried off, could not be made good by any catch."[144] As we have seen, Pliny believed the ends justified the cost of the "hook" or he would not have invested the funds required. A successful business manager can only make a similar determination when an investment opportunity is properly defined and the milestones for success are fully delineated.

6 - Pliny's Outcome

The Importance of Pliny's Flexibility

Pliny concluded his letter to Calvisius Rufus both by sharing the positive reception he received for his innovative plan as well as recapping the rationale for his actions (demonstrating not only his pride but also his understanding of his audience and mastery of his medium of communication); however, the most striking word in this concluding sentence's translation is "novelty":

> "The whole district is praising the novelty of my rebate and the way in which it was carried out and the people I classified and graded instead of measuring all with the same rod, so to speak, have departed feeling obliged to me in proportion to their honest worth and satisfied that I am not a person who 'holds in equal honor the wicked and the good.'"

The concept of novelty was critical to Pliny's program. Pliny had created a new approach to dealing with rebates and it received wide acclaim. Pliny the businessman was not wedded to custom or the status quo; he sought an innovative solution that worked. This flexibility on Pliny's part is somewhat surprising given his very classical Roman education that valued tradition and seemed to disdain change.

The Paradoxical Pliny

Pliny even described his own learning process when he was commenting upon the shortcomings of the younger generation and wrote "it was the recognized custom for us to learn from our elders by watching their behavior as well as listening to their advice."[145] Pliny, like all of his class, was a man steeped in tradition so it is somewhat paradoxical

Entrepreneurship and Ethics in Ancient Rome

that he explored such an entrepreneurial solution to his business problem. This was not the only instance where Pliny pursued a creative approach to a problem. In a letter complaining about long-term issues with his tenant farmers, Pliny said "I must make the experiment and try all possible changes of remedy for an obstinate complaint."[146]

Pliny, never an iconoclast, surprisingly showed serious inclinations toward nonconformity and not just in the business space. In one of his very late letters written before leaving for Bithynia, Pliny advised a literary friend: "It may be safer to keep to the plain but the road lies too low to be interesting."[147] Regardless of the origin of Pliny's apparently late blooming affection for risk (perhaps it was related to Pliny's acceptance of his distant and last assignment), it is extremely important to understand that Pliny's success as a businessman depended upon his ability to be sufficiently flexible to explore novel solutions to his business problems. This brings us to our final lesson obtained from Epistle 8.2.

Lesson 20: Remain Open to New Ideas

Pliny revealed his flexibility in dealing with the frustration of his buyers and demonstrated a willingness to innovate. The result was an imaginative incentive program conceived and implemented in a way that generated district-wide praise for Pliny. It should be pointed out, however, that if Pliny had been absent from the estate at harvest time, it is doubtful that a local bailiff would have dared to take any action other than what was minimally required. The actual implementation of

6 - Pliny's Outcome

an innovative idea requires both knowledge of the situation and a degree of authority.

Although Pliny in the past had shown a willingness to delegate, such as for construction purchases, one can imagine that a financial micromanager such as Pliny would not have been pleased if a subordinate had taken the initiative to unilaterally issue any type of rebates to the grape buyers. Pliny himself recognized the risks that often fell upon subordinates when he reminded a correspondent that it is not uncommon that "the influential might make scapegoats of the humble."[148] Such a complex rebate plan would not have been successfully designed and implemented if Pliny had not been at the estate to personally deal with the buyers' frustration.

M. I. Finley found that the lack of innovation on ancient Roman farms was specifically due to the absentee landlord and concluded that the landlord "represents the viewpoint of the policeman not of the entrepreneur."[149] Finley added that "customary methods allowed for technical refinements – this must be said repeatedly – but normally stopped there."[150] Unfortunately, this prejudice against change also appears to have extended as high as the Emperors.

Example of Resistance to Change—Tiberius

In our discussion of knowing your audience in Lesson 16, we saw the entrepreneurial glassmaker misread the Emperor Tiberius and, as a result, literally lose his head. Looking at the meeting from the Emperor's perspective, we see a leader predisposed to avoiding risk, losing any economic

Entrepreneurship and Ethics in Ancient Rome

benefit that might have accrued from the invention of a new form of glass. Tiberius embraced the status quo, not innovation.

Figure 6.2: Shows a gold aureus depicting the Emperor Tiberius,[151] a ruler who embraced the status quo and who typically resisted change. (Courtesy of Classical Numismatic Group, Inc. http://www.cngcoins.com)

Example of Resistance to Change - Vespasian

Tiberius, who tended to avoid change in almost all spheres of his governance, was not alone in his fear of economic change. We also see the same sort of distaste from the Emperor Vespasian. Vespasian, under whose reign (69-79 AD) the Coliseum in Rome (see Figure 6.3) had first begun,[152] required the transport of columns for another building project. Although cranes (see Figure 6.4) would not have been uncommon at major construction sites, Suetonius wrote: "To a mechanical engineer, who promised to transport heavy columns to the Capitol at small expense, he (Vespasian) gave no mean reward for his invention."[153] Vespasian, unlike Tiberius, treated the entrepreneurial engineer with respect but Suetonius went on to say that the

6 - Pliny's Outcome

emperor told the engineer: "You must let me feed my poor commons"[154] and rejected the use of the engineer's device for low cost transport.

Figure 6.3: Shows an early photograph of the Coliseum[155] whose construction was begun under the Emperor Vespasian.

Figure 6.4: Shows a modern rendering of an ancient Roman construction crane[156].

Entrepreneurship and Ethics in Ancient Rome

Figure 6.5: Shows an aureus depicting the Emperor Vespasian[157] who treated an entrepreneurial transport engineer with respect, unlike Tiberius and his treatment of the innovative glassmaker. (Courtesy of Classical Numismatic Group, Inc. http://www.cngcoins.com)

Pliny the Exception

Pliny was very much the exception in an environment that placed an extraordinary value on tradition and very little on innovation. The environment in which Pliny conducted his business differed greatly from the modern business world, where agents of change and innovation are cultivated and admired. Unfortunately, despite the rhetoric about change, true innovators are far too infrequently found. Where they do cast, they are often smothered by the stultifying bureaucracy of large enterprises or by the often overly-restrictive policies found at all levels of government. There simply needs to be greater effort when it comes to incubating innovation.

The entrepreneur, however, should never lose heart and remain resolute; rather, he or she should always anticipate risk, analyze risk and adjust for risk when required. Pliny's rebate plan appears

6 - Pliny's Outcome

(based on Pliny's description in his letter) to have been successfully implemented exactly as conceived but we cannot be certain that the plan did not undergo some "tweaking" as it was implemented. Pliny may have made some adjustments to avoid failure and simply chose not to mention them – we just cannot know for certain.

Risk and Risk Mitigation

A modern innovator cannot assume that the execution of an idea will flow as flawlessly as Pliny's conceptualization and execution of his rebate program; therefore, the entrepreneur must be prepared for the eventuality that a concept and its implementation may require some degree of adjustment over time. Modifications can range from minor to major but the key is to be prepared for as many risks as can be reasonably identified. One means for accomplishing this is with a risk register, a simple modeling tool that allows for the categorization and weighting of risks along with planned responses for each risk.

To demonstrate how such a risk mitigation strategy can be constructed and implemented, a sample risk register for Pliny's rebate plan is provided in Figure 6.6. Based on Pliny's Letter 8.2, the rebate plan proceeded with Plinian perfection and so adjustments in the program were unnecessary but such perfection in the ordinary course of business should never be expected and certainly should never be relied upon.

147

Entrepreneurship and Ethics in Ancient Rome

Risk Description	Impact	Probability	Potential Responses
Buyer Rebates Insufficient	High	Medium	Increase Payouts to Buyers
Rebate Excessive Compared to Crop Value	Medium	Low	Decrease Payouts to Buyers or Pliny Absorbs Additional Costs
Program Viewed as Unduly Complex	Low	High	Improve Buyer Communications
Pliny's Peers View Rebate Program as Wasteful/Foolish	High	Low	Curtail Communication of Program

Figure 6.6: A sample risk register for risks that could have impacted the success of Pliny's rebate program's rollout.

Chapter Conclusion

With this lesson, we have completed the chapter on the outcome of Pliny's actions and learned of the successful implementation of Pliny's complex scheme of rebates. In this chapter, we also saw that Pliny's program was well received by the grape buyers and facilitated the creation of the final two lessons from Pliny's Epistle 8.2:

- Lesson 19: Delineate Investment Objectives
- Lesson 20: Remain Open to New Ideas

We saw earlier that Pliny completed his letter to Calvisius Rufus with a recap of his reasons for implementing his rebate program and we should do no less here with the twenty lessons of Plinian Management:

6 - Pliny's Outcome

- Lesson 1: Promote your Successes
- Lesson 2: Establish Rigorous Standards for Advisors
- Lesson 3: Align the Message with the Medium
- Lesson 4: Self-Deprecate in Difficult Situations
- Lesson 5: Manage Crises in Person
- Lesson 6: Fully Evaluate Transactional Risks
- Lesson 7: Avoid Single Sourcing
- Lesson 8: Encourage Competition Amongst Partners
- Lesson 9: Remember Business is Personal
- Lesson 10: Be Fair in Business Transactions
- Lesson 11: Cultivate an Ethical Business Reputation
- Lesson 12: Fully Understand your Constraints
- Lesson 13: Ignore Complex Solutions at your own Risk
- Lesson 14: Incent your Partners
- Lesson 15: Micromanage your Capital
- Lesson 16: Know your Audience
- Lesson 17: Closely Monitor Receivables
- Lesson 18: Build Long-Term Buyer Relationships
- Lesson 19: Delineate Investment Objectives
- Lesson 20: Remain Open to New Ideas

Entrepreneurship and Ethics in Ancient Rome

CHAPTER 7

Pliny's Lessons

Pliny, as discussed in the introduction, made a claim that he was making a collection of his letters as they came into his hands, which we have seen that he did not. On the other hand, the twenty lessons reviewed in this text and summarized in the last chapter are discussed in the order they arose from the content of Pliny's Epistle 8.2; however, the order of the lessons, from a traditional management viewpoint, is somewhat random. We should take one final look at the lessons obtained from Pliny's management approach with the lesson order revised based on the similarity of topics.

When we regroup the lessons, we see that they fit very well within a taxonomy consisting of four key management constructs that should be much more recognizable to the aspiring entrepreneur or manager of today. Once regrouped, the Plinian Management Lessons reveal just how well Pliny's approach to his business challenges applies to today's business needs and form a very solid

Entrepreneurship and Ethics in Ancient Rome

foundation upon which to base a business career. It should be noted, however, that these constructs are not an exhaustive list of areas that affect the operation of a modern enterprise and exclude such important areas as raising capital, product development and revenue generation, to name just a few.

After reviewing each of the four sets of lessons, I have added selected insights of Peter Drucker, the well-known business management consultant and teacher who *Businessweek* magazine called "The Man Who Invented Management". [158] The addition of Professor Drucker's comments provides an opportunity to compare the key management themes that have emerged from Pliny's ancient lessons with those of the greatest management theorist of the modern era.

Business Leadership

The first grouping highlights business leadership and includes Pliny's core set of lessons that deal with ethics, business relationships and innovation:

- Lesson 9: Remember Business is Personal
- Lesson 10: Be Fair in Business Transactions
- Lesson 11: Cultivate an Ethical Business Reputation
- Lesson 18: Build Long-Term Buyer Relationships
- Lesson 20: Remain Open to New Ideas

7 - Pliny's Lessons

These leadership lessons business clearly reflect the importance Pliny placed on ethical business practices and the importance of avoiding rigidity in one's decision making. Professor Drucker, commenting on leadership, reminds us of the huge chasm between truly being a business leader and just managing: "Management is doing things right; leadership is doing the right things."[159] Pliny as we saw time and time again was obsessed with doing the right things (and also doing things right) and his lessons fit comfortably within Drucker's leadership paradigm.

Financial Management

The second grouping of Plinian Management Lessons stresses the criticality of solid financial management and also includes risk analysis and partner management:

- Lesson 6: Fully Evaluate Transactional Risks
- Lesson 8: Encourage Competition Amongst Partners
- Lesson 15: Micromanage your Capital
- Lesson 17: Closely Monitor Receivables
- Lesson 19: Delineate Investment Objectives

Pliny's lessons in financial management emerged from carefully husbanding his personal resources and those of the Emperor. In the modern business world, a typical manager has his or her focus on company assets but for the entrepreneur, personal and business assets are most often the same. Drucker, like Pliny, clearly emphasized the importance of asset management when he wrote "Management's duty is to preserve the assets of the institution in its care."[160] When responsible for the money of others, there is an even greater obligation to "do the right things" than there is with one's own capital. That obligation was very consistently evident in Pliny's outlook and actions.

Personal Advancement

The third group of lessons focuses on techniques that assist in personal advancement and cover the topics of self-promotion, personnel management and communications:

- Lesson 1: Promote your Successes
- Lesson 2: Establish Rigorous Standards for Advisors
- Lesson 3: Align the Message with the Medium
- Lesson 4: Self-Deprecate in Difficult Situations
- Lesson 14: Incentivize your Partners

The Plinian lessons in personal advancement are by their nature tactical – they are part of the necessary steps in a career progression. Drucker provides a supplement to our Plinian Lessons here when he reminds ambitious managers that the

> *"critical factor for success is accountability – holding yourself accountable. Everything else flows from that. The important thing is not that you have rank but that you have responsibility."*[161]

7 - Pliny's Lessons

Pliny's ethical approach to his decisions repeatedly demonstrated the sense of responsibility and accountability demanded by Drucker's admonition that one's advancement never should compromise one's obligations to others.

Problem Management

Our fourth and final set of lessons emphasizes key aspects of problem management and covers the topics of crisis management, constraints and solution generation:

- Lesson 5: Manage Crises in Person
- Lesson 7: Avoid Single Sourcing
- Lesson 12: Fully Understand your Constraints
- Lesson 13: Ignore Complex Solutions at your own Risk
- Lesson 16: Know your Audience

We clearly saw that Pliny worked to successfully manage his way through his business problems and also attempted to avoid future crises. Crises, however, cannot always be averted. When they come, Drucker reminds us of our most important task when managing through difficult periods: "In turbulent times, the first task of management is to make sure of the institution's capacity to survive a blow."[162] Pliny's entrepreneurial actions helped insulate his Tuscan estate from any catastrophic damage from the short-term impact of collapsing grape prices and allowed Pliny to not only survive the "blow" but also to improve the probability of the long term survival of his grape buyers and hence his market, as well.

Entrepreneurship and Ethics in Ancient Rome

Pliny's Ethical Standards

We have seen that Pliny's lessons dovetail closely with the management and leadership outlook of the modern world's most respected management authority: Peter Drucker. The real value of Pliny's lessons only emerges in their application and it is in the application process that the aspiring entrepreneur and business manger will understand the extent to which Pliny established a gold standard in ethical business management.

In the introduction, I wrote of my late-developing affinity for Pliny and the surprise I felt to see that my management style was reflective of Pliny's. Pliny attempted to set himself up as an ethical role model for his readers, just as I have positioned him for mine. I must frankly admit that I do not always live up to the Plinian ideals expressed in these lessons but I do feel that I always try my best and hope for no less from my readers. We must simply recognize that Pliny's ethical standards were impossibly high, perhaps higher than he could have even realistically met anywhere other than within his own letters.

Pliny's Benchmark for Success

As we saw earlier, Pliny was well aware that his ultimate success and reputation would be judged by future generations of readers of his letters. In that respect, we are perhaps more fortunate than Pliny for our success needs only to be judged by conscience and the company's bottom line. Pliny clearly had the tougher challenge, especially given that the principate greatly limited his opportunity for personal success and renown, as it did for all citizens of Rome, especially the upper classes. Pliny

7 - Pliny's Lessons

was left with a very limited canvas with which he could create a lasting portrait of himself. Pliny himself lamented about that limitation when he wrote to a friend: "You want me to follow Cicero's example but my position is very different from his. He was not only richly gifted but was supplied with a wealth of varied and important topics to suit his abilities, though you know without my telling you the narrow limits confining me."[163] Though Cicero may have lived in a more exciting time than Pliny, Cicero, despite his fame, was executed during the unrest that emanated from the fall of the Roman Republic following Caesar's murder. Pliny may have wished to emulate Cicero in all things but we can reasonably assume that such an end for himself as Cicero suffered (decapitation along with the severing of his hands for writing his orations against Mark Antony[164]), was surely not what Pliny would have actually lamented missing.

There is, however, some degree of truth in Pliny's frustration in finding a means for achieving greatness. Pliny was no Cicero (as much as he may have wished to be so) but he was an extraordinary administrator, as evidenced by his continued usefulness to three Emperors. Unfortunately, the poets write no ballads thanking the administrator for his or her noble contributions to the state or recite tales of great and courageous deeds of administration. Pliny well recognized the challenge of achieving lasting administrative greatness. Hence Pliny's determination to publish his letters in hopes that posterity anointed him with literary immortality.

Entrepreneurship and Ethics in Ancient Rome

Pliny Praised and Pummeled

Pliny's letters have indeed successfully left a Pliny legacy but unfortunately that legacy is pummeled as often as it is praised. For example, Julian Bennett does both in his recent biography, *Trajan Optimus Princeps*. Bennett is extremely appreciative of Pliny's documentary insights into Trajan's regime and called Pliny's first nine books "invaluable, providing essential evidence which exists nowhere else for the organization of Roman civil and state bureaucracy, legal procedure and the rural economy..."[165] However, Bennett then proceeds to follow the praise with the pummeling of the man. Bennett concludes: "The first nine books of the Letters expose Pliny as a rather Pickwickian character. He is fond of himself and his doings, ... equally at home in Club and Pub."[166] With regard to Pliny's tenth book of letters to Trajan, Bennett effuses that they are "...unrivalled as a source..."[167] but then complains that these very letters reveal that Pliny too frequently referred decisions back to the emperor seeking direction and that "Pliny stands as an unmitigated temporizer."[168]

Pliny was again correct in his assessment of his audience — it has always been very difficult to be honored as an administrative superstar and it seems that imperial biographers, like their subjects, are also never satisfied. What seems to bedevil historians and literary scholars alike about Pliny is the very essence of what made him a successful businessman — the day-to-day dogged determination to complete the often-unexciting task at hand, to do so in an ethical fashion and to be recognized for its accomplishment.

7 - Pliny's Lessons

Pliny the Literary Innovator

A retired imperial secretary[169] once advised Pliny that he should write history. Pliny, in his response, declined to follow a path so well traveled by others, perhaps fearful that he was not up to the task and would struggle to complete any such work to his own high standards. Pliny also went on to comment "anything left unfinished might as well not have been begun."[170] It would have been out of character if Pliny, amongst his many virtues, did not possess an obsessive commitment for completing what he began to the best of his ability. It is also very likely that Pliny, the innovator, declined out of a determination to create a new literary genre[171] an autobiography based upon the publication of his letters.

Pliny's Managerial Legacy Nearly Lost

The modern manager could do much worse than emulating Pliny's determination, both to complete any task once started and to pursue opportunities that create a separation from one's competitors. Perhaps nothing shows the benefit of such determination better than Pliny commenting to Tacitus that, during the eruption of Mt. Vesuvius, he returned to his studies while Vesuvius belched it murderous plumes into the sky. Pliny wrote that Pliny the Elder "saw at once that it (Vesuvius' eruption) was important enough for a closer inspection and he ordered a fast boat to be made ready, telling me I could come with him if I wished. I replied that I preferred to go on with my studies."[172] What other seventeen-year-old boy than Pliny would pass on an invitation to watch at close quarters a volcano erupt and doggedly choose to study instead?

Entrepreneurship and Ethics in Ancient Rome

Pliny did pass up the opportunity though, a decision for which he is being reproved in Figure 7.1 below. This was wise for otherwise he might have perished along with his inquisitive uncle.

It is quite possible that there was a part of Pliny that might have wished for the same glorious death as Pliny the Elder but fortunately for us it that was not his destiny. If Pliny had dramatically perished during the Vesuvius cataclysm instead of quietly passing in Bithynia, history would have been the poorer for we would not have had the Letters of the Younger Pliny. We would have missed Pliny's insights into the golden age of Rome and we would have lost the entrepreneurial and ethical lessons gained from Pliny's approach to the management of his Tuscan grape growing business.

Figure 7.1: Print by Thomas Burke of Pliny being reproved for not leaving his studies to investigate the eruption of Mt. Vesuvius with his uncle Pliny the Elder.[173] *Pliny the Elder, appointed Prefect of the Navy by the Emperor Vespasian, initially intended to investigate the cataclysm but ultimately perished in his efforts to assist in the evacuation those endangered by the eruption.*

APPENDIX A

Pliny's Bio

Although Pliny began his rise to power and influence under the Emperor Domitian (81-96 AD), it was during the reigns of the Emperors Nerva (from 96-98 AD) and Trajan (from 98-117 AD) that Pliny's career flourished and reached its apex with the consulship, Rome's highest administrative office under the emperors. In order to properly place Pliny amongst the aristocrats of ancient Rome, we must first understand the magnitude of Pliny's wealth. The unit of money used throughout this text, a sesterce (also shown as HS 1) may be thought of as buying $4.00 of value today based on the modern value of gold.[174]

In Pliny's day a Roman legionnaire could have earned HS 1,200 annually[175] while Pliny's earnings from his estates is estimated[176] at HS 1.1 million annually. Pliny's overall wealth is placed at HS 20 million and included one or two Tuscan villas, "a townhouse in Rome, a suburban seaside villa 17 miles from Rome ... and at least three villas on Lake

Entrepreneurship and Ethics in Ancient Rome

Como (near modern Milan), making a total of not less than six or seven houses in all."[177]

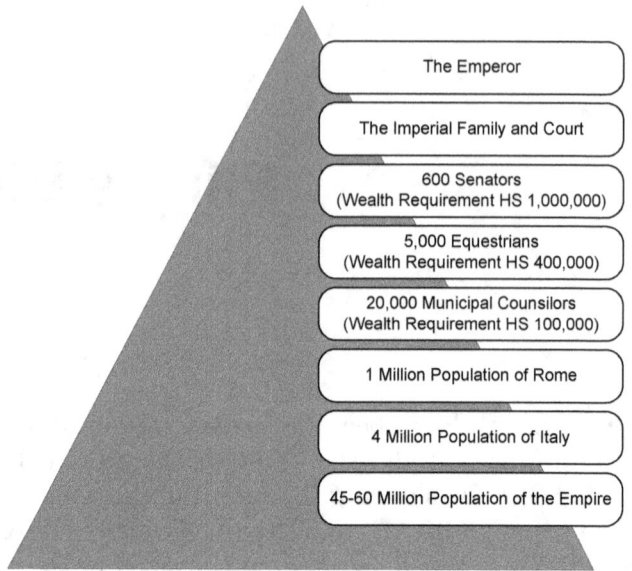

Figure A.1: shows the highly stratified tiers of the Roman society in which Pliny, as a Senator and Consul, functioned. Clearly, Pliny sat comfortably amongst Rome's elite both politically and financially.

Pliny's Early Life

Pliny was born in Comum (modern Como, near present day Milan) into a well-to-do equestrian family (aristocratic, but junior to Senators) while Nero was still emperor. Pliny's father, of which little is known, died while Pliny was still young but Pliny's maternal uncle, Pliny the Elder, helped to raise Pliny. Pliny the Elder was a well-connected wealthy equestrian who served as an advisor to the Emperor Vespasian, providing Pliny an early tutorial in how to serve an emperor.[179]

Appendix A - Pliny's Bio

Figure A.2: Shows an 1834 Painting of Pliny's hometown of Comum (modern Como) by Jean-Baptiste Camille Corot.[180]

Pliny the Elder was so close to the imperial family that he dedicated his encyclopedic Natural History to Titus, Vespasian's elder son and successor as emperor. Upon his death the Elder Pliny bequeathed to the younger Pliny the lucrative Tuscan estate that generated an estimated 400,000 sesterces annually[181] and whose problems are the focus of this text. (See Appendix E for Pliny's description of his Tuscan estate.) In his will, the Elder Pliny also adopted the younger Pliny as his son (this type of testamentary adoption was not uncommon among the elite of ancient Rome).

Entrepreneurship and Ethics in Ancient Rome

Figure A.3: A reconstruction of Pliny's Tuscan Estate by Karl Friedrich Schinkel based upon the descriptions of the villa in Pliny's letters.[182]

Pliny's Education and Elevation to the Senate

Clearly, Pliny's family could well afford the cost of a first class education in Rome which, in fact, Pliny obtained under Quintilian, "the greatest rhetorician in Roman history, a man who held a chair endowed by the emperor (Vespasian) and from whom Pliny acquired a love of language and literature."[183] Pliny was unsurprisingly studious and began[184] at age eighteen to argue cases at the Centumviral Court.[185] As a young man, he would surely have seen the great Coliseum of Rome rise and dominate the skyline. With his wealth, family background and an uncle's imperial connections, Pliny was well positioned for appointment to the Senate[186] and the Emperor Domitian (Vespasian's younger son who became emperor upon his older brother Titus' early death) did elevate Pliny to the Senate when he supported Pliny's candidacy in 87 AD.

Appendix A - Pliny's Bio

The Emperor's support meant that Pliny was elected without competition to the position of quaestor, a junior administrative position that brought with it entry into the Roman Senate.[187] As quaestor, Pliny would have had some responsibility for administrating state taxes and finances, apparently showing an early expertise that would be greatly appreciated by future emperors.

Figure A.4: Shows a marble Bust of the "bad" Emperor Domitian. Domitian appointed Pliny to the Senate.[188]

Entrepreneurship and Ethics in Ancient Rome

Pliny's Career Progression and Financial Acuity

Pliny steadily advanced in his career, eventually holding two successive senior financial positions. We need not just assume that Pliny possessed financial skill and enthusiasm that uniquely qualified him for these positions because we find proof of his financial acuity throughout his letters and even in his will, which partially survives in a fragmentary inscription now in a wall of the Church of St. Ambrose in Milan. A portion of the inscription reads:[189]

> "left by (Pliny's) will public baths ... and an additional 300,000 sesterces for furnishing them, with interest on 200,000 for their upkeep... to his city ... 1,866,666 2/3 sesterces to support a hundred of his freedmen and subsequently to provide an annual dinner for the people of the city..." (Appendix F contains a complete translation of the sections of Pliny's will that survive.)

This inscription provides us two key insights into Pliny's character. First Pliny reveals that he was a very generous individual. Supporting examples from Pliny's letters referenced throughout this text will also reinforce this observation as to Pliny's munificence. Pliny's generosity was in fact so extraordinary that M. I. Finley, in his classic *The Ancient Economy* noted "the benefactions of the younger Pliny, (were) probably unsurpassed in Italy or the western empire."[190]

Second, the inscription emphasizes specific donation amounts, even including fractional sesterces, revealing Pliny's passion for financial detail. Duncan-Jones in his *The Economy of the*

Appendix A - Pliny's Bio

Roman Empire notes "the irregularity of the capital sum is very unusual among Roman endowments. It probably results from Pliny wanting to apply a particular rate of benefit per head for the support of his freedmen."[191] This unique enthusiasm for complex financial calculation also appears in a number of Pliny's letters. Pliny's financial skills must have also been clearly evident to the Emperors of his day for we see that the two senior financial positions occupied by Pliny included significant and broad responsibilities for state finances.

The first financial appointment for Pliny by Domitian in 94 AD was prefect for military finances, overseeing military pensions for three years, which was followed by his appointment in 98 AD as prefect for the state treasury by the Emperor Nerva following Domitian's assassination.[192] Both positions required financial expertise and the fact that two Emperors — one — demonized (Domitian) and the other deified (Nerva) called upon his services unequivocally demonstrates that Pliny's important positions in state finance were not due to nepotism or mere chance but rather due to competence recognized at the pinnacle of Roman government.

Entrepreneurship and Ethics in Ancient Rome

Figure A.5: Shows a marble bust of the "good" Emperor Nerva. Nerva, following Domitian's assassination, appointed Pliny to the position of prefect for the state treasury.[193]

Pliny's Elevation to Roman Consul

Nerva's successor, Trajan, perhaps in recognition of Pliny's dedicated service to the state in his prior positions, elevated Pliny to the office of consul when Pliny was 40 years old. During the Roman republic, the office of consul was the most powerful administrative and military position in the state[194] and was at one time or another held by such legendary Romans as Julius Caesar, Pompey the Great, Marcus Crassus and Cicero. However, by Pliny's day, the Emperors had reduced this once powerful office to little more than a ceremonial position, conferring great honor and status but little

Appendix A - Pliny's Bio

else. Despite this, the honor was so great that the achievement of the position of consul was still the culmination of many careers.

Additionally, for a few talented and well-connected men, the position of consul could open even further appointments by the emperor, as occurred in Pliny's case. Trajan, in 103 AD, followed Pliny's term as consul with his appointment to a senior post in the Roman priesthood: augur. Pliny was thrilled with the appointment once held by his hero, Cicero, and wrote of it: "the priesthood is an old established religious office and has a particular sanctity in that it is held for life."[195] Pliny, comparing himself to Cicero, went on to brag: "As I have reached the same priesthood and consulship at a much earlier age than he (Cicero) did, I hope I may attain something of his genius at least in later life."[196] However, the ever-practical Pliny quickly emerged barely two sentences later in the same letter: "such genius is difficult to achieve and almost too much to hope for; it can only be granted by the gods."[197]

Figure A.6: Marble Bust of Cicero, Pliny's hero and role model.[198]

Entrepreneurship and Ethics in Ancient Rome

Pliny's Additional Imperial Assignments

The Emperor Trajan, however, was still not finished with Pliny and selected him for three additional assignments. The first, again demonstrating the Emperor's confidence in Pliny, was to serve as an assessor providing advice to Trajan himself during an imperial inquiry.[199] The second assignment, with a three-year duration, was for Pliny to oversee the Tiber River Conservancy Board, being responsible for keeping the riverbanks in repair to reduce the risk of the Tiber's flooding. Such flooding occurred sometime after Pliny left the position and Pliny wrote of the damage to a friend with the seasoned eye of an experienced professional: "The Tiber has overflowed its bed and deeply flooded its lower banks so that, although it is being drained by the canal cut by the Emperor, with his usual foresight, it is filling the valleys and inundating the fields and wherever there is level ground there is nothing to be seen but water."[200] Pliny then went on to describe the human and property damage from the storm as befitted a former custodian of the Tiber's riverbanks. An additional important duty of Pliny's while he was in that custodial position was responsibility for the maintenance of Rome's sewer systems.

Responsibility for Rome's safety and cleanliness may not have been particularly exciting but one can assume, given Pliny's practical outlook and the detailed damage reporting in the above letter, that Pliny performed his duties with diligence and effectiveness. More than half a century earlier, when still a youth, the future emperor Vespasian failed in his job of keeping the streets of Rome clean and the emperor at the time, Caligula, "ordered that he be covered with mud, which the soldiers heaped

Appendix A - Pliny's Bio

into the bosom of his purple-bordered toga."[201] Given Caligula's violent nature, Vespasian was lucky to be reproved so gently; however, the anecdote clearly reveals the importance with which the emperors, even the unstable ones, viewed these types of administrative positions.

Pliny's Final Imperial Assignment

The final assignment given to Pliny by Trajan was as special envoy of the emperor to the province of Bithynia-Pontus (part of modern day Turkey) in Asia Minor (see Figure A.8). The province was a financial mess and Trajan wanted Pliny, who also had experience with the Bithynians in the courts, to clean it up. This would be the last appointment of Pliny's career and of his life for Pliny died in 112 AD (or possibly 113 AD), just two years into the assignment at the age of 51 or 52.

Despite Pliny's early death, his correspondence with the Emperor Trajan, most written during his assignment in Bithynia-Pontus, was preserved and likely published shortly after Pliny's death. These letters, along with other correspondence written from approximately[202] 96 AD to 108 AD, provide a simultaneously rich yet somewhat sanitized documentation of Pliny's character, life and times. Henderson, in his *Pliny's Statue*, describes Pliny's letters as providing an insight into Pliny's Rome that is "an incomparably valuable databank for the detail and texture of social life."[203]

Entrepreneurship and Ethics in Ancient Rome

Figure A.7: Shows a marble bust of the Emperor Trajan. Pliny's correspondence with Trajan provides a rich insight into Trajan's imperial administration that, according to the historian Edward Gibbon, was conducted with "virtue and abilities" (see Appendix C).[204]

Appendix A - Pliny's Bio

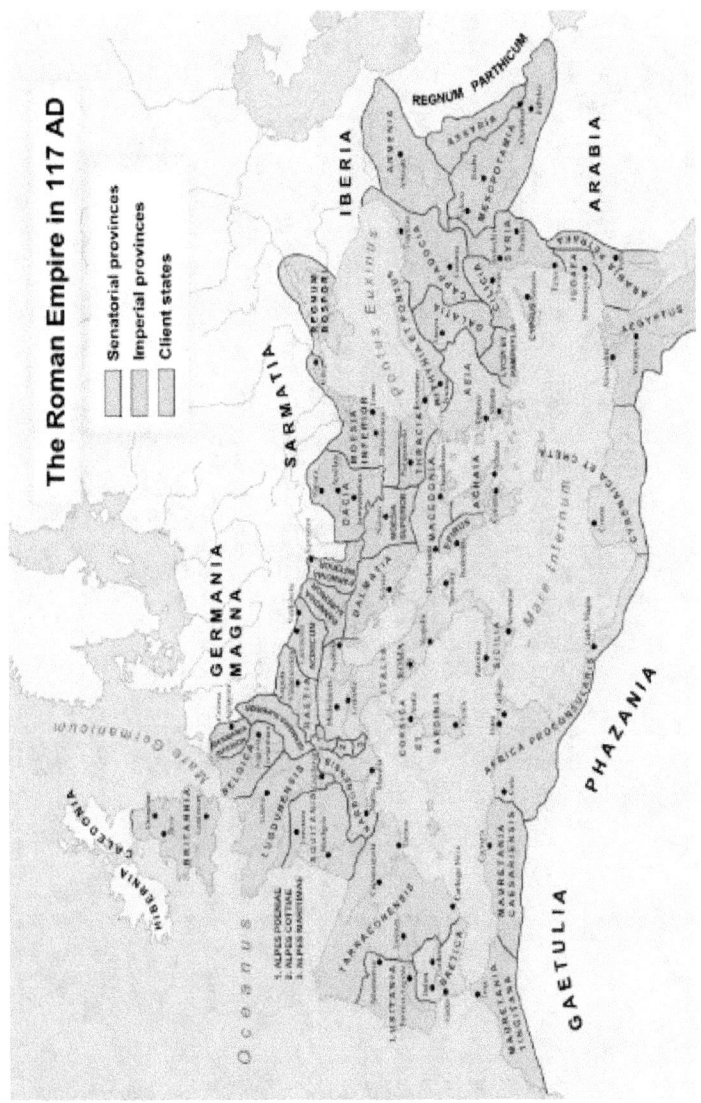

Figure A.8: This map[205] shows the extent of the Roman Empire in 117 AD during the reign of the Emperor Trajan. Pliny's final assignment for Trajan was to serve as an Imperial Envoy in Bithynia-Pontus, part of modern day Turkey.

Entrepreneurship and Ethics in Ancient Rome

Figure A.9: This map of ancient Italy[206] shows Pliny's birthplace of Comum (Como), ancient Pompeii and the imperial capital Roma (Rome). Pliny's Tuscan estate was near the ancient town of Tifernum Tiberinum in Umbria on the Tiberis (Tiber) nestled in the foothills of the Appenninus (Apennines). Map courtesy of the Ancient World Mapping Center © 2012 (www.unc.edu/awmc)

Appendix A - Pliny's Bio

Pliny's Personal Interests

From Pliny's letters, we learn of Pliny's love for his wife Calpurnia[207] (she was possibly his second or third wife), his frustration that he was childless, his enjoyment of the tranquility of his estates, his passion for literature (especially his efforts at penning it), and even of his patronage of the poet Martial. We also learn that, in addition to Pliny's affection for financial computation, he greatly desired — even obsessed with ensuring — that his fame continued in perpetuity.

Pliny was very blunt about constructing such a legacy through the written word:

> "Create something, perfect it to be yours for all time; for everything else you possess will fall to one or another master after you are dead but this will never cease to be yours once it has come into being."[208]

Pliny, one of the foremost politicians and orators of his day, craved literary fame, perhaps realizing that this was the best means for him to succeed in establishing an enduring reputation. Pliny informed a correspondent that literary success was in his blood: "My uncle (Pliny the Elder), who was also my father by adoption, was a historian, ... and I find it an excellent thing to follow in the footsteps of one's forebears ..."[209]

Pliny's Literary Aspirations

Pliny's longing to emulate Cicero, not just in the political arena but also in the world of letters, intensified his desire to achieve literary renown. Pliny unabashedly wrote "I am so anxious to make him (Cicero) my model in my literary work."[210] Perhaps this is why Pliny was so pleased that the poet Martial, a client of Pliny's to whom Pliny provided financial support, wrote an epigram of him. Despite some risqué verses, Pliny willingly[211] included portions of the poem in a letter to a friend commiserating Martial's death.

Martial's key lines for Pliny's purposes were that "all the hours of his working day he (Pliny) devotes to crabbed Minerva (the Roman goddess of wisdom pictured in Figure A.10)"[212] and "while he works up for the 200 ears of the high court, something the ages and generations to come may well bracket with the tracts of Arpinum's star."[213] Arpinum (now Arpino in central Italy) was the birthplace of Cicero and so for Martial to write that for generations to come, Pliny's works would be bracketed by "the tracts of Arpinum's star" Cicero, could only have immensely gratified Pliny, his patron.

Unfortunately, Martial overreached just a bit for as Professor Henderson points out with regard to Pliny's literary aspirations, Pliny "is one of those authors who forever appears but on the edge of classical canon."[214] Regardless of the placement of Pliny in the literary world, the value of his letters to historians is extraordinary and Pliny's counsel for the student of business is invaluable as well. As we have seen from his career progression, Pliny's professional responsibilities and experiences were not that far removed from those of a modern business manager wrestling with the financial challenges of today.

Appendix A - Pliny's Bio

Figure A.10. This bronze bust of Minerva, the Roman Goddess of Wisdom, dates to Pliny's time. Pliny referenced this goddess numerous times in his letters.

Entrepreneurship and Ethics in Ancient Rome

APPENDIX B

Pliny's Comments on his Readership

"I have often had all the applause my heart could desire; but never have I felt such pleasure as I did recently at something Tacitus said. He was describing how at the last Races he had sat next to a Roman knight who engaged him in conversation on several learned subjects and then asked if he came from Italy or the provinces. 'You know me,' said Tacitus, 'from your reading.' At which the man said, 'then are you Tacitus or Pliny?' I can't tell you how delighted I am to have our names assigned to literature as if they belonged there and not to individuals and to learn that we are both known by our writing to people who would otherwise not have heard of us.

A similar thing happened to me a day or two ago. I had a distinguished neighbor to dinner, Fadius Rufinus, and on his other side was someone from his native town who had come to Rome for the first visit that same day. Pointing to me, Rufinus said to him, 'Do you see that friend here?' Then he spoke at length about my work and the man exclaimed, 'It must be Pliny!'"[215]

Entrepreneurship and Ethics in Ancient Rome

APPENDIX C

Pliny's Times

One of the most famous descriptions of Pliny's times comes from the great British historian Edward Gibbon who, in 1776, began the first of his seven-volume masterpiece, *The History of the Decline and Fall of the Roman Empire,* with the following description of the Roman Empire at its greatest:

> "In the second century of the Christian era, the empire of Rome comprehended the fairest part of the earth and the most civilized portion of mankind. The frontiers of that extensive monarchy were guarded by ancient renown and disciplined valour. The gentle but powerful, influence of laws and manners had gradually cemented the union of the provinces. Their peaceful inhabitants enjoyed and abused the advantages of wealth and luxury. The image of a free constitution was preserved with decent reverence. The Roman senate appeared to possess the sovereign authority and devolved on the emperors all the executive powers of government."[216]

This was the Rome of Pliny, a Rome at her zenith.

Entrepreneurship and Ethics in Ancient Rome

APPENDIX D

First Century Emperors

Emperor	Reign
Augustus	31 BC – 14 AD
Tiberius	14 AD – 37 AD
Caligula	37 AD – 41 AD
Claudius	41 AD – 54 AD
Nero	54 AD – 68 AD
Galba	68 AD – 69 AD
Ortho	69 AD
Vitellius	69 AD
Vespasian	69 AD – 79 AD
Titus	79 AD – 81 AD
Domitian	81 AD – 96 AD
Nerva	96 AD – 98 AD
Trajan	98 AD – 117 AD

Entrepreneurship and Ethics in Ancient Rome

APPENDIX E

Pliny's Tuscan Vineyard

"Picture to yourself a vast amphitheatre such as only could be the work of nature; the great spreading plain is ringed round by mountains, their summits crowned by ancient woods of tall trees, where there is a good deal of mixed hunting to be had. Down the mountain slopes are timber woods interspersed with small hills of soil so rich that there is scarcely a rocky outcrop to be found; these hills are fully fertile as the level plain and yield quite a rich harvest, though it ripens later in season. Below them the vineyards spreading down every slope weave their uniform pattern far and wide, their lower limit bordered by a plantation of trees. Then come the meadows and cornfields ... (with) the river Tiber flowing through the fields. The river is navigable, so that all produce is conveyed to Rome by boat...

My house is on the lower slope of a hill but commands a good view as if it were higher up, for the ground rises gradually that the slope is imperceptible and you find yourself at the top without noticing the climb. Behind it is the Apennine range, though some ways off... "[217]

Entrepreneurship and Ethics in Ancient Rome

APPENDIX F

Pliny's Will

"Gaius Plinius Caecilius Secundus, son of Lucius of the tribe Oufentina, consul: augur: praetorian commissioner with full consular power for the province of Pontus and Bithynia, sent to that province in accordance with the Senate's decree by the Emperor Nerva Trajan Augustus, victor over Germany and Dacia, the Father of his Country: curator of the bed and banks of the Tiber and sewers of Rome: official of the Treasury of Saturn: official of the military treasury: praetor: tribune of the people: quaestor of the Emperor: commissioner of the Roman knights: military tribune of the Third Gallic legion: magistrate on the board of Ten: left by will public baths at the cost of . . . . and an additional 300,000 sesterces for furnishing them, with interest on 200,000 for their upkeep. . . . and also to his city capital of 1,866,666 2/3 sesterces to support a hundred of his freedmen and subsequently to provide an annual dinner for the people of the city . . . . Likewise in his lifetime he gave 500,000 sesterces for the maintenance of boys and girls of the city and also 100,000 for the upkeep of the library..."[218]

Entrepreneurship and Ethics in Ancient Rome

Appendix G

Endnotes

Chapter 1

[1] Pliny Letters 8.2.1. All quotations of Pliny's letters, unless noted otherwise, are taken from Radice.

[2] Sherwin-White (page 448)

[3] Erdman (pages 124-5); The term "problematic harvest" is used extensively in this text; however, the actual problem in this case is not with the harvest per se but rather the financial impact of declining grape prices, which is discussed at length in Chapter 3.

[4] Pliny Letters 6.16 and 6.20

[5] Pliny Letters 10.96

[6] Pliny Letters 10.96.8

[7] See *Riding the Runaway Horse* by Charles Kenny, 1992

[8] Carlon (page 9)

[9] Pliny Letters 1.1.1

[10] Hoffer (page 24)

[11] Prof. Carlon pointed out the importance of the dating of Pliny's Tribunate and Praetorship to the author.

[12] Courtesy of Classical Numismatic Group, Inc. http://www.cngcoins.com

[13] Courtesy of Classical Numismatic Group, Inc. http://www.cngcoins.com

[14] Courtesy of Classical Numismatic Group, Inc. http://www.cngcoins.com

[15] This image (or other media file) is in the public domain because the copyright has expired.

Chapter 2

[16] Suetonius *Lives of the Caesars* 8.7.2

[17] Suetonius *Lives of the Caesars* 2.42.1

[18] This image (or other media file) is in the public domain because the copyright has expired.

[19] Pliny *Natural History* 14.17.97. All quotations of Pliny the Elder's *Natural History* are taken from Rackham (Books 12-16), Jones (Books 28-32) and Eichholz (Books 36-37).

[20] Pliny Letters 8.2

[21] Pliny Letters 1.8.14

[22] Pliny Letters 1.8.15

[23] Henderson (page 1)

Endnotes

[24] Henderson (page 1)

[25] Beard (page 1)

[26] Suetonius *Lives of the Caesars* 1.37.2

[27] This image (or other media file) is in the public domain. Source: Tataryn77. http://en.wikipedia.org/wiki/File:CaesarTusculum.jpg.

[28] "The baker, his tomb, his wife and her breadbasket: the monument of Eurysaces in Rome." Lauren Hackworth Petersen. *The Art Bulletin*. College art Association. 2003. AccessMyLibrary. Accessed 4 Jan. 2010. (http//www.accesmylibrary.com).

[29] Zanker (page 15)

[30] Petersen (page 3)

[31] This image (or other media file) is in the public domain. Source: Joris van Rooden on 03-01-2006. http://en.wikipedia.org/wiki/File:P.Maggiore_Tomb.JPG.

[32] Joshel (page 163)

[33] Joshel (page 166)

[34] Petersen (page 16)

[35] Pliny Letters 10.13.1

[36] Sherwin-White (pages 448-450)

[37] Pliny Letters 2.20.1

[38] Pliny Letters 3.19.1

Entrepreneurship and Ethics in Ancient Rome

[39] Pliny Letters 3.2.3

[40] Sherwin-White (page 739)

[41] Pliny Letters 2.12.6

[42] *The New American Bible* (Page 645)

[43] Uetonius *Lives of the Caesars* 2.87.1

[44] Everitt (page 232)

[45] Richard (page 58)

[46] Pliny Letters 7.25.6

[47] Cicero To Atticus 5.1. All quotations of Cicero's letters are taken from Shackleton Bailey.

[48] Cicero To Atticus 28.1

[49] Pliny Letters 10.45.1

[50] Pliny Letters 10.120.1

[51] According to Suetonius in Book 2.49.3, the Imperial Post, which capitalized on Rome's outstanding system of roads, was created by the Emperor Augustus: "to enable what was going on in each of the provinces to be reported and known more speedily and timely."

[52] Carlon (page 10)

[53] Plutarch Cicero 24.2. All quotations of Plutarch's *Lives* are taken from Clough.

Endnotes

Chapter 3

[54] *Quintilian Institutes of Oratory* 9.29 (Watson)

[55] Pliny Letters 8.15.2

[56] Cicero To Atticus 363.1

[57] Pliny Letters 10.8.5

[58] Pliny Letters 10.8.6

[59] Sherwin-White (page 270)

[60] Pliny Letters 4.6.1

[61] Pliny Letters 4.6.2

[62] Sherwin-White (page 39

[63] Sherwin-White (page 39)

[64] Cicero To Atticus 317.2

[65] Pliny Letters 3.6.5

[66] Pliny Letters 9.39

[67] Cicero To Atticus 363.1

[68] Pliny Letters 9.20.2

[69] Sherwin-White (page 519); Erdkamp (page 124)

70. Murphy, Dean E. (2003, May 25) "California Grape Rush of 90's Withers as Prices Collapse New York Times". Retrieved from http://www.nytimes.com/2003/05/25/us/california-grape-rush-of-90-s-withers-as-prices-collapse.html?pagewanted=all&src=pm

71. Cato *On Agriculture* (page 131). All quotations of Cato's *On Agriculture* are taken from Hooper.

72. Pliny *Natural History* 14.5.50

73. Younger (page 166)

74. Church (page 368)

75. Petronius *The Satyricon* 5.53. All quotations of Petronius' *The Satyricon* are taken from Arrowsmith.

76. Erdkamp (page 110)

77. Younger (page 177)

78. Pliny *Natural History* Book 14.3.10

79. Peterson (page 6)

80. Petronius *The Satyricon* 5.76

81. Courtesy of BPM Wine. http://bpmwine.blogspot.com/. Of the 168 respondents, 93% were in CA and 82% were integrated grape growers and vintners while just 18% were grape growers.

82. Erdkamp (page 125)

83. Pliny Letters 3.19.4

Endnotes

[84] Sherwin-White (page 302)

[85] Pliny Letters 4.24.6

[86] Pliny Letters 5.4.3

[87] Sherwin-White (page 253)

[88] Erdkamp (pages 118-120)

[89] Erdkamp (page 120)

[90] Pliny *Natural History* 31.43.93

[91] Curtis (page 716S)

[92] Curtis (page 716S)

[93] Curtis (page 716S)

[94] Picture from the Villa of Aulus Umbricius Scaurus, Pompeii. Source: Claus Ableiter. Wikipedia. Web. Accessed 24 Feb. 2012. <http://en.wikipedia.org/wiki/File:Garum_Mosaik_Pompeji.JPG>.

[95] Cato *On Agriculture* (page 131)

[96] Erdkamp (page 123)

[97] Andreau (page 149)

[98] Petronius *The Satyricon* 5.38

[99] Pliny Letters 9.36.6

[100] Pliny Letters 9.15.1

[101] Pliny Letters 1.24.2

Entrepreneurship and Ethics in Ancient Rome

¹⁰² Sherwin-White (page 160)

¹⁰³ Pliny Letters 2.11.6

Chapter 4

¹⁰⁴ Sherwin-White (page 450)

¹⁰⁵ Miller (page 153)

¹⁰⁶ Jones (page 172)

¹⁰⁷ Plutarch *Crassus* 2.4

¹⁰⁸ This image (or other media file) is in the public domain. Source: http://en.wikipedia.org/wiki/File:Marcus_Licinius_Crassus.

¹⁰⁹ Pliny Letters 5.7.5

¹¹⁰ Pliny Letters 3.20.8-9

¹¹¹ Pliny Letters 2.20.12

¹¹² Pliny Letters 5.1.3

¹¹³ Pliny Letters 9.3.1

¹¹⁴ Pliny Letters 10.9.1

¹¹⁵ Plutarch *Crassus* 1.2

¹¹⁶ Dio Cassius 40.27.3. All quotations of Dio Cassius' *Roman History* are taken from Cary.

¹¹⁷ Pliny Letters 6.22.7

¹¹⁸ *The New American Bible* (page 1124)

Chapter 5

[119] Bennett (page 81)

[120] Harris (pages 22-23)

[121] Pliny Letters 8.24.6

[122] Cicero *On Duties* 1.42.150. All quotations of Cicero's On Duties are taken from Miller.

[123] Pliny Letters 10.43.1-2

[124] Sherwin-White (page 129)

[125] Pliny Letters 1.19.2

[126] Sherwin-White (page 288)

[127] Pliny Letters 4.13.8

[128] Petronius *The Satyricon* 5.38

[129] Pliny Letters 1.20.2

[130] This image (or other media file) is in the public domain. Source: http://en.wikipedia.org/wiki/File:Tiberius.

[131] Pliny *Natural History* 28.5.23

[132] Petronius *The Satyricon* 5.51

[133] Pliny *Natural History* 36.66

[134] Pliny Letters 3.18.3

Entrepreneurship and Ethics in Ancient Rome

[135] At this point Pliny's program no longer resembles a quantity discount as discussed in Lesson 14 and has morphed into a full-blown incentive plan. We should also note that if prices did vary amongst the buyers, Pliny would likely have addressed the issue within the rebate structure, which he did not do.

[136] Pliny Letters 9.37.1-2

[137] Finley (page 92)

Chapter 6

[138] Pliny Letters 1.8.6

[139] Pliny Letters 2.4.3

[140] Pliny Letters 10.54.1-2

[141] Finley (page 117)

[142] Finley (page 117)

[143] Sherwin-White (pages 449-450)

[144] Suetonius *Lives of the Caesars* 2.25.4

[145] Pliny Letters 8.14.4

[146] Pliny Letters 9.37.4

[147] Pliny Letters 9.26.2

[148] Pliny Letters 3.9.9

[149] Finley (page 113)

[150] Finley (page 114)

Endnotes

[151] This image (or other media file) is in the public domain. Source: Tataryn77. http://en.wikipedia.org/wiki/File:TiberiusAureus.jpg.

[152] The Coliseum was completed in the reign of the Emperor Titus.

[153] Suetonius *Lives of the Caesars* 8.18.1

[154] Suetonius *Lives of the Caesars* 8.18.1

[155] This image (or other media file) is in the public domain because the copyright has expired. Source: Library of Congress, Prints and Photographs Division. http://www.flickr.com/photos/library_of_congress/4755211528/

[156] Courtesy of TurboSquid.

[157] Courtesy of Classical Numismatic Group, Inc. http://www.cngcoins.com

Chapter 7

[158] John A. Byrne, with Lindsey Gerdes. "The Man Who Invented Management." Bloomberg/Businessweek. Novemeber 28, 2005. Accessed February 24, 2012. http://www.businessweek.com/magazine/content/05_48/b3961001.htm

[159] The Drucker School, Claremont Graduate University. www.cgu.edu/PDFFiles/Drucker/MBA_brochure.pdf. 20 February 2012.

[160] Drucker (page 9)

[161] Drucker (page 177)

Entrepreneurship and Ethics in Ancient Rome

[162] Drucker (page 368)

[163] Pliny Letters 9.2.2

[164] Plutarch *Cicero* 48.4

[165] Bennett (page 133)

[166] Bennett (page 133)

[167] Bennett (page 133)

[168] Bennett (page 117)

[169] Sherwin-White (page 333)

[170] Pliny Letters 5.8.7

[171] Carlon (page 2)

[172] Pliny Letters 6.16.7

[173] This image (or other media file) is in the public domain because the copyright has expired.

Appendix A

[174] This estimate is based upon the following assumptions: one sesterce (HS 1) was valued at 1/100th of a gold coin called an aureus that weighed 7.3 grams during Nero's reign and one Troy oz. weighing 31 grams is today valued at approximately $1,700. Therefore, HS 1 can be thought equivalent to $4. A different gold valuation or commodity comparison (e.g. silver, wheat, etc.) would yield a different value relationship.

[175] Jones (page 172)

Endnotes

[176] Scheidel (page 207)

[177] Duncan-Jones (page 23)

[178] Jones (2006), (page 172)

[179] The importance of young Pliny's early exposure to imperial service was pointed out to the author by Professor Carlon.

[180] This image (or other media file) is in the public domain because the copyright has expired. Source: The Yorck Project: 10.000 Meisterwerke der Malerei. DVD-ROM, 2002. ISBN 3936122202. Distributed by DIRECTMEDIA Publishing GmbH. http://en.wikipedia.org/wiki/File:Jean-Baptiste-Camille_Corot_044.jpg.

[181] Sherwin-White (page 70)

[182] This image (or other media file) is in the public domain because the copyright has expired. Source: Karl Friedrich Schinkel, *Architektonisches Album*, 1842.

[183] Wilken (page 3)

[184] Radice (Vol. 1, page x)

[185] The court adjudicating property and inheritance cases.

[186] Wilken (page 2)

[187] Sherwin-White (page 74)

[188] This image (or other media file) is in the public domain. Source: Jastrow (2006). http://en.wikipedia.org/wiki/File:Bust_Domitian

189 Radice (Vol. 1; 549)

190 Finley (page 39)

191 Duncan-Jones (page 30)

192 Wilken (page 5)

193 This image (or other media file) is in the public domain. Source: Jastrow (2006). http://en.wikipedia.org/wiki/File:Nerva.

194 It was under Julius Caesar's adopted son and first emperor, Augustus Caesar, that the role of consul began its slide into figurehead status.

195 Pliny Letters 4.8.1

196 Pliny Letters 4.8.5

197 Pliny Letters 4.8.6

198 This image (or other media file) is in the public domain because the copyright has expired.

199 Pliny Letters 4.22.1

200 Pliny Letters 8.17.1-2

201 Suetonius *Lives of the Caesars* 8.5.3. All quotations of Suetonius' *Lives of the Caesars* are taken from Rolfe.

202 Sherwin-White (page 41)

203 Henderson (page x)

Endnotes

[204] This image (or other media file) is in the public domain. Source: User:Bibi Saint-Pol. http://en.wikipedia.org/wiki/File:Traianus_Glyptothek_Munich_336.jpg

[205] This image (or other media file) is in the public domain. Source: Andrei nacu at en.wikipedia. http://en.wikipedia.org/wiki/File:RomanEmpire_117.svg.

[206] Courtesy of the Ancient World Mapping Center © 2012 (www.unc.edu/awmc)

[207] Carlon (note 41, page 165) notes that the historical emergence of the love letter genre can be credited to Pliny and his letters to his young wife Calpurnia; see also Sherwin-White pages 405-407.

[208] Pliny Letters 1.3.4-5

[209] Pliny Letters 5.8.5

[210] Pliny Letters 4.8.4-5

[211] Henderson (page 47)

[212] Pliny Letters 3.21.5

[213] Henderson (page 50)

[214] Henderson (page x)

Appendix B

[215] Pliny Letters 9.23; also in Letter 1.2 Pliny writes: "the books which I have already sent out into the world are still said to find readers..."

Appendix C

[216] Gibbon (page 5)

Appendix E

[217] Pliny Letters 5.6

Appendix F

[218] Radice (Appendix A, Vol. II, page 551)

Appendix H

Bibliography

Ancient Sources

Arrowsmith, William (trans.), (1987), *The Satyricon / Petronius*. New York: The Penguin Group.

Church, Alfred John and Brodribb, William Jackson (trans.) (1982). *The Annals of Tacitus*. Franklin Center: The Franklin Library.

Cary, Earnest (trans.), (2005), *Dio Cassius, Roman History*. Vol. III. Cambridge: Harvard University Press.

Clough, Arthur Hugh (trans. and ed.), (2001), *Plutarch's Lives* (intro. by Atlas, J.). Vols. I and II. New York: Random House, Inc.

Eichholz, D. E. (trans.), (2001), *Pliny's Natural History.* Vol. X. Cambridge: Harvard University Press.

Forster, F. S. and Heffner, Edward, H. (trans.), (1968), *Columella On Agriculture.* Vol. III Cambridge: Harvard University Press.

Hooper, W. D. and Ash, H. B. (trans.), (2006), *Cato On Agriculture and Varro On Agriculture.* Cambridge: Harvard University Press.

Jones, W. H. S (trans.), (2000), *Pliny's Natural History.* Vol. VIII. Cambridge: Harvard University Press.

Miller, Walter (trans.) (2005), *Cicero, On Duties.* Cambridge: Harvard University Press.

Perrin, Bernadotte, (trans.), (1916), *Plutarch's Lives, Crassus.* Vol. III. Cambridge: Harvard University Press.

Perrin, Bernadotte, (trans.), (1919), *Plutarch's Lives, Cicero.* Vol. VII. Cambridge: Harvard University Press.

Rackham, H. (trans.), (2005), *Pliny's Natural History.* Vol. IV. Cambridge: Harvard University Press.

Radice, Betty, (trans.), (1969), *Pliny's Letters and Panegyricus.* Vols. I and II. Cambridge: Harvard University Press.

Radice, Betty, (trans. and intro.), (1986), *The Letters of Pliny the Younger*. New York: Penguin Books.

Rolfe J. C., (trans.), (2001), *Suetonius* (intro. by Bradley, K. R.) Vols. I and II. Cambridge: Harvard University Press.

Shackleton Bailey, D.R. (ed. and trans.), (1999), Cicero, *Letters to Atticus*. Vols. I and IV. Cambridge: Harvard University Press.

Walsh, P.G. (trans.), (2006), *Pliny the Younger, Complete Letters*. Oxford: Oxford University Press.

Watson, Rev. John Selby, (trans.), (1856 rep.), *Quintilian's Institutes of Oratory*, Vol.2. London: Henry G. Bohn.

Secondary Sources

Andreau, J. (1999), *Banking and Business in the Roman World*. Cambridge: Cambridge University press.

Beard, Mary (2007), *The Roman Triumph*. Cambridge: The Belknap Press of Harvard University.

Bennett, Julian (1997), *Trajan, Optimus Princeps*. Bloomington: Indiana University Press.

Birley, A. R. (2000), *Onomasticon to Younger Pliny*. Leipzig: K. G. Saur Munchen.

Entrepreneurship and Ethics in Ancient Rome

Birley, Anthony (trans. and intro.) (1976), *Lives of the Later Caesars, The first part of the Augustan History, with Newly Compiled Lives of Nerva and Trajan.* London: Penguin Books

Byrne, John A. and Gerdes, Lindsey. "The Man Who Invented management." Bloomberg/ Businessweek. Novemebr 28, 2005. *http://www.businessweek.com/ magazine/content/05_48/b3961001. htm* Accessed February 24, 2012.

Carlon, Jacqueline M. (2009), *Pliny's Women, Constructing Virtue and Creating Identity in the Roman World.* Cambridge: Cambridge University Press.

Curtis, Robert I. (September 2009): "Umami and the foods of Classical Antiquity." American Journal of Clinical Nutrition, doi: 10.3945/ajcn.2009.27462C Vol. 90, No. 3, pp. 712S-718S.

Drucker, Peter F. and Maciariello, Joseph A. (2004), *The Daily Drucker.* New York: HarperCollins.

Duncan-Jones, Richard. (1982), *The Economy of the Roman Empire, Quantitative Studies.* Cambridge: Cambridge University Press.

Du Prey, Pierre de la Ruffinière. (1994), *The Villas of Pliny From Antiquity to Posterity.* Chicago: The University of Chicago Press.

Bibliography

Erdkamp, Paul (2005), *The Grain Market in the Roman Empire, A social, political and economic study*. Cambridge: Cambridge University Press.

Everitt, Anthony (2003), *The Life and Times of Rome's Greatest Politician, Cicero*. New York: Random House.

Finley, M. I. (1999), *The Ancient Economy* (w. foreword by Morris, I.) Berkeley: California University Press.

Finley, M. I. (Feb. 2000), *Technological Innovation and Economic Progress in the Ancient World. The Economic History Review,* New Series, Vol.53, No. 1, pp. 29-59. Published by: Blackwell publishing on behalf of the Economic History Society.

Gibbon, Edward (1909 ed. Reprinted in 1974), *The History of the Decline and Fall of the Roman Empire*. Vol.1 New York: AMS Press.

Grainger, John D. (2004), *Nerva and the Roman Succession Crisis of AD 96-99*. New York: Routlidge.

Grant, Michael (1970), *The Ancient Historians*. New York: Barnes and Noble, Inc.

Green, Kevin, (Feb. 2000): "Technological innovation and economic progress in the ancient world: M. I. Finley re-considered." *The Economic History Review,* New Series, Vol.53, No. 1, pp. 29-59. Published by: Blackwell publishing on behalf of the Economic History Society.

Entrepreneurship and Ethics in Ancient Rome

Harris, W. V. (ed) (1993): "The Inscribed Economy, Production and distribution in the Roman empire in the light of instrumentum domesticum". Ann Arbor: *Journal of Roman Archeology*, Supplementary Series Number Six

Henderson, John (2002), *Pliny's Statue, The Letters, Self-Portraiture and Classical Art.* Exeter: University of Exeter Press.

Hill, H (1974), *The Roman Middle Class in the Republican Period.* Westport: Greenwood Press.

Hoffer, S.E. (1999), *The Anxieties of Pliny the Younger.* Atlanta: Scholar Press

Jones, Brian W. (1993) *The Emperor Domitian.* London: Routledge.

Jones, David (2006), *The Bankers Of Puteoli, Finance, Trade and Industry in the Roman World.* Gloucestershire: Tempus Publishing Limited.

Joshel, Sandra (1992), *Work, Identity and Legal Status at Rome, A study of Occupational Inscriptions.* Norman: University of Oklahoma Press.

Kenny, Charles (1992), *Riding the Runaway Horse.* Boston: Little Brown & Co.

Levick, Barbara (1999), *Vespasian.* London: Routledge.

Marchesi, Ilaria (2008), *The Art of Pliny's Letters* (Kindle Edition). Cambridge University Press.

Bibliography

Moreley, Neville (2007), *Trade in Classical Antiquity*. Cambridge: Cambridge University Press.

Murphy, Dean E. (2003, May 25). "California Grape Rush of 90's Withers as Prices Collapse. New York Times." Retrieved from http://www.nytimes.com/2003/05/25/us/california-grape-rush-of-90-s-withers-as-prices-collapse.html?pagewanted=all&src=pm

Nicholson, John. "The Delivery and Confidentiality of Cicero's Letters." *The Classical Journal*, Vol. 90, No. 1 (Oct.- Nov., 1994), pp. 33-63.

Petersen, Lauren Hackworth. "The baker, his tomb, his wife and her breadbasket: the monument of Eurysaces in Rome." *The Art Bulletin*. College art Association. 2003. AccessMyLibrary. 4 Jan. 2010 (http//www.accesmylibrary.com)

Prag, Jonathan and Repath, Ian (2009), *Petronius, A Handbook*. West Sussex: Wiley-Blackwell.

Richard, Carl J., (1994), *The Founders and the Classics, Greece, Rome and the American Enlightenment*. Cambridge: Harvard University Press.

Rostovtzeff, Michael. "The Problem of the Origin of Serfdom in the Roman Empire." *The Journal of Land & Public Utility Economics*, Vol.2, No. 2 (Apr., 1926), pp. 198-207. The University of Wisconsin Press Journals Division.

Sampson, Gareth, C. (2008), *The Defeat of Rome in the East, Crassus, The Parthians and the Disastrous Battle of Carrhae, 53BC*. Drexel Hill: Casemate.

Scheidel, Walter and Von Reden, Sitta (eds.), (2002), *The Ancient Economy*. New York: Routledge.

Sherwin-White, A.N. (1966), *The Letters of Pliny: a Historical and Social Commentary*. Oxford: The Claredon Press.

The Drucker School, Claremont Graduate University. www.cgu.edu/PDFFiles/Drucker/MBA_brochure.pdf. 20 February 2012.

The New American Bible (1981). Wichita: Fireside Bible Publishers.

Younger, William (1966), *God, Men and Wine*. Cleveland: The Wine and Food Society in association with World Publishing Company.

Wilken, Robert L. (1984), *The Christians as the Romans Saw Them*. New Haven: Yale University Press.

Zanker, Paul (1990), (Shapiro, Alan, trans.), *The Power of Images in the Age of Augustus*. Ann Arbor: The University of Michigan Press.

Index of Ancient Names and Places

A

Agrippa, 28

Apennine. *See Appenninus*

Appenninus, 174, 185

Arpino. *See Arpinum*

Arpinum, 58, 176

Asia Minor, 22, 38, 171

Athens, 48

Atista, 40

Atticus, 48, 54, 58, 59

Augustus, 28-29, 46-47, 119, 140, 183

Aulus Umbricius Scaurus. *See Scaurus*

B

Bithynia, 22, 49, 99, 142, 160, 171, 173, 187

C

Caesar, 23, 30, 38-39, 42, 46, 55, 58, 89, 157, 168

Caligula, 23, 170-171, 183

Calpurnia, 175

Calvisius Rufus, 13, 20, 30, 32, 34-35, 37, 43-44, 47, 50, 52-53, 61, 67, 69, 71, 91, 105, 111, 116, 125, 131, 133, 141, 148

Campania, 64

Carrhae, 94

Cato, 46-47, 62

Cato the Elder, 62, 78

Chios, 30

Cicero, 22-23, 48-49, 51, 54-55, 58-60, 88, 110, 157, 168-169, 175-176

Claudius, 41, 183

Columella, 133, 136, 137

Comum, 24, 43, 47, 52, 107, 162-163, 174

Crassus, 89-91, 94, 168

D

Dacia, 187

Dio Cassius, 94

Domitian, 23, 25, 28, 161, 164-165, 167-168, 183

Index

E
Egypt, 44
Eurysaces, 39-42, 64

F
Fadius Rufinus, 179

G
Gaius Julius Proculus, 79, 115
Gaius Plinius Caecilius Secundus, 13, 22. *Also see Pliny*
Galba, 183
Germany, 187

H
Herculaneum, 76

I
Italy, 28, 30, 64, 166, 174

J
Jericho, 99
Jesus, 15, 99-101
Judea, 100, 119
Julius Caesar. *See Caesar*
Julius Proculus. *See Gaius Julius Proculus*
Juvenal, 42

L

Lesbos, 30

Lucius Junius Moderatus Collumella. *See Columella*

Luke, 99

M

Marcus Crassus. *See Crassus*

Marcus Vegilius Eurysaces. *See Eurysaces*

Mark Antony, 157

Martial, 175-176

Minerva, 176-177

Mt. Vesuvius, 15, 159-161

N

Nero, 63, 162, 183

Nerva, 23, 25, 161, 167-168, 183

O

Ortho, 183

Oufentina, 187

P

Petronius, 63, 79, 110, 115, 118-120, 125

Pliny

  and Christians, 15

  and Mt. Vesuvius, 15, 159-161

Index

birth, 15, 22, 162

death, 22, 171

education, 24, 164

epistle 8.2, 30-32

personal interests, 24, 175

resume, 22-24

Lesson 1: Promote your Successes, 38
Lesson 2: Establish Rigorous Standards for Advisors, 44-45
Lesson 3: Align the Message with the Medium, 48-49
Lesson 4: Self-deprecate in Difficult Situations, 54-55
Lesson 5: Manage Crises in Person, 58
Lesson 6: Fully Evaluate Transactional Risks, 66-67
Lesson 7: Avoid Single Sourcing, 72
Lesson 8: Encourage Competition Amongst Partners, 79-80
Lesson 9: Remember Business is Personal, 81-82
Lesson 10: Be Fair in Business Transactions, 87-88
Lesson 11: Cultivate an Ethical Business Reputation, 93
Lesson 12: Fully Understand your Constraints, 98-99
Lesson 13: Ignore Complex Solutions at your own Risk, 107
Lesson 14: Incent your Partners, 109-110
Lesson 15: Micromanage your Capital, 113
Lesson 16: Know your Audience, 117-118
Lesson 17: Closely Monitor Receivables, 122-123
Lesson 18: Build Long-term buyer Relationships, 126-127
Lesson 19: Delineate Investment Objectives, 139
Lesson 20: Remain Open to New Ideas, 142-143

Pliny the Elder, 15, 29, 62, 64, 112, 119-120, 159-160, 162-163, 175

Pliny the Younger. *See Pliny*

Plutarch, 51, 94

Pompeii, 15, 77, 174

Pompey the Great, 23, 168

Pomponius. *See Atticus*

Pontius Pilate, 117

Pontus. *See Bithynia*

Proculus. *See Gaius Julius Proculus*

Q

Quintilian, 24, 54, 164

R

Roma. *See Rome*

Rome, 13, 16, 21-24, 29, 33, 35, 38-39, 48, 50, 56, 62-63, 79, 89, 92, 94, 123, 131, 144, 156, 160-161, 163-164, 170, 174, 179, 181, 185, 187

S

Scaurus, 76-77

Sicily, 30

Suetonius, 15, 28, 38, 82, 119, 140, 144

Syria, 24, 94

St. Paul, 15

Index

St. Peter, 15

T

Tacitus, 14-15, 63, 117, 119, 159, 179
Tiber, 22, 170, 174, 185, 187
Tiberis, 174
Tiberius, 118-119, 143-144, 146, 183
Tifernum, 174
Titus, 164, 183
Trajan, 14-15, 22-23, 25-26, 43, 49, 55-56, 93, 112, 132, 158, 161, 168-173, 183, 187
Trimalchio, 64
Turkey, 22, 171, 173
Tuscany, 13, 57, 79

U

Umbria, 174

V

Vespasian, 144-146, 161, 162, 164, 170-171, 183
Vestorius, 59
Vitellius, 183

Z

Zacchaeus, 99-102

Entrepreneurship and Ethics in Ancient Rome

About the Author

Bob is a retired business executive whose career spanned more than 30 years in the high tech industry. Bob began his professional career at Xerox Corporation after he obtained a Bachelor of Science degree in Physics from Worcester Polytechnic Institute and an MBA from the University of Rochester's Simon School of Business. In 1980 Bob joined Wang Laboratories and spent twenty years with Wang and its successor companies in a variety of product development, marketing, sales and service management positions. Following Wang's emergence from bankruptcy in 1993 as Wang Global, Bob was named President of Wang Canada and following his turnaround of that operation, Bob

Entrepreneurship and Ethics in Ancient Rome

was appointed President of Wang Global's North American Field Service operation with responsibility for over 4,000 employees and revenues of more than half a billion dollars.

In 2000, following Getronics NV's acquisition of Wang Global, Bob led a management buyout of a division of Getronics and was appointed President and CEO of QualxServ, the newly formed company. Under Bob's leadership QualxServ grew into a global computer services provider spanning more than a dozen countries and employing over 3,000 computer service professionals worldwide.

After spending nearly a decade with QualxServ, Bob retired from his position as President and CEO in 2009 and stepped down from QualxServ's Board in 2010 (the company has since been renamed Worldwide TechServices). Retirement has allowed Bob to spend more time with his wife Diane and daughters Meredith and Allison as well as pursue his passion for the study of the business management lessons that can be learned from ancient Rome.

Bob remains a consultant to Worldwide TechServices, serves as an Advisor to Work Market, a web-based labor management company and is a member of both the Simon School of Business Advisory Council and the George Eastman Circle at the University of Rochester.

LESSONS FROM
HISTORY

About the Series

This series is for primarily business and IT professionals looking for inspiration for their projects. Specifically, business managers responsible for solving business problems, or Project Managers (PMs) responsible for delivering business solutions through IT projects.

This series uses relevant historical case studies to examine how historical projects and emerging technologies of the past solved complex problems. It then draws comparisons to challenges encountered in today's IT projects.

This series benefits the reader in several ways:

- It outlines the stages involved in delivering a complex IT project providing a step-by-step guide to the project deliverables.

- It vividly describes the crucial lessons from historical projects and complements these with some of today's best practices.

- It makes the whole learning experience more memorable.

The series should inspire the reader as these historical projects were achieved with a lesser (inferior) technology.

Website: http://www.lessons-from-history.com/

Did you like this book?

If you enjoyed this book, you will find more interesting books at

www.MMPubs.com

Please take the time to let us know how you liked this book. Even short reviews of 2-3 sentences can be helpful and may be used in our marketing materials. If you take the time to post a review for this book on Amazon.com, let us know when the review is posted and you will receive a free audiobook or ebook from our catalog. Simply email the link to the review once it is live on Amazon.com, with your name and your mailing address—send the email to orders@mmpubs.com with the subject line "Book Review Posted on Amazon."

If you have questions about this book, our customer loyalty program, or our review rewards program, please contact us at info@mmpubs.com.

Oshawa, Ontario, Canada

Project Lessons from the Roman Empire: An Ancient Guide to Modern Project Management

The leaders of the Roman Empire established many of the organizational governance practices that we follow today, in addition to remarkable feats of engineering using primitive tools that produced roads and bridges which are still being used today, complex irrigation systems, and even "flush toilets." Yet, the leaders were challenged with political intrigue, rebelling team members, and pressure from the competition. How could they achieve such long-lasting greatness in the face of these challenges?

In this new addition to the Lessons from History series, join author Jerry Manas as he takes you on a journey through history to learn about project management the Roman way. Discover the 23 key lessons that can be learned from the successes and failures of the Roman leadership, with specific advice on how they can be applied to today's projects.

Read this intriguing book to learn how they did it.

ISBN-13:   9781554890545   (paperback)

Available in print and electronic formats. Order from your local bookseller, Amazon.com, or directly from the publisher at **www.mmpubs.com**.

The History of Project Management

The Pyramid of Giza, the Colosseum, and the Transcontinental Railroad are all great historical projects from the past four millennia. When we look back, we tend to look at these as great architectural or engineering works. Project management tends to be overlooked, and yet its core principles were used extensively in these projects.

Mark Kozak-Holland explores the history of project management and how it evolved over the past 4,500 years. This book shows that "modern" project management practices did not just appear in the past 100 years but have been used — often with a lot of sophistication — for thousands of years.

As readers explore the many case studies in this book, they will discover fascinating details of innovative projects that produced many of our most famous landmarks and voyages of discovery.

ISBN-13:   9781554890965   (Hardcover)

Available in print and electronic formats. Order from your local bookseller, Amazon.com, or directly from the publisher at **www.mmpubs.com**.

Churchill's Adaptive Enterprise: Lessons for Business Today

Winston Churchill is widely regarded as one of the greatest leaders of the 20th century. But as he became Prime Minister in May 1940, in a period of calamitous change, what did he actually do? How did he transform his organization to turn his perilous situation around?

As he illustrates Churchill's journey to an Adaptive Enterprise, author Mark Kozak-Holland draws parallels between events in World War II and today's business challenges.

Churchill created his Adaptive Enterprise in a very dire situation. Not only did the transformed organization work, but it surpassed all expectations and changed the course of history. This book will show you how he did it, and how you can do the same in your own organization.

ISBN-13:   9781895186192   (Paperback)

Available in print and electronic formats. Order from your local bookseller, Amazon.com, or directly from the publisher at **www.mmpubs.com**.

Project Management Blunders: Lessons from the Project that Built, Launched, and Sank Titanic

White Star's initiative to build its new Olympic-class ships can be described as a text book project. It started off very well in the initiation and planning phases: the project team had a very good understanding of the business and customer needs, a solid vision, a superlative business case, the right supplier partnerships, good stakeholder relationships, and a healthy balance of proven and emerging technologies.

By the end of the design phase, however, decisions were made that compromised safety features. By the end of the fitting-out phase, all key stakeholders believed that the ships could never founder.

Mark Kozak-Holland reveals the project management blunders that doomed *Titanic* while it was still being built. Filled with photos and copies of actual documents from the project, this book walks you through a case study in project management failure.

ISBN-13:   9781554891221   (paperback)

Available in print and electronic formats. Order from your local bookseller, Amazon.com, or directly from the publisher at **www.mmpubs.com**.

Titanic Lessons in Project Leadership: Effective Communication and Team Building

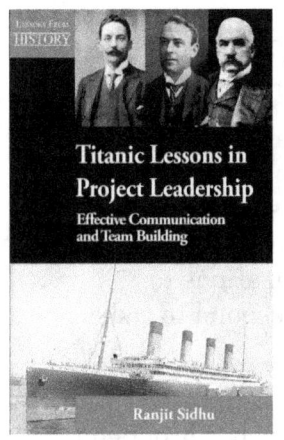

In *Titanic Lessons in Project Leadership* we see how "small" and easily overlooked behavioral and communication issues can aggregate through a project to become seemingly unthinkable errors.

This book focuses on the people aspects of the *Titanic* story; the key stakeholders, power dynamics, underlying perceptions, communication, leadership and team interactions. Ranjit Sidhu draws on this tragic tale to focus on the "behind the scenes" aspects of human communication and leadership to guide you in the right direction for making that vital difference to your current projects.

Combining contemporary management theory with her own insights and extensive project management experience, Ranjit offers practical guidance and lessons from history that will help you gain a deeper understanding of how leaders and teams can operate at their very best.

ISBN-13:   9781554891207   (paperback)

Available in print and electronic formats. Order from your local bookseller, Amazon.com, or directly from the publisher at **www.mmpubs.com**.

Polaris: Lessons in Risk Management

Risk management is one of the most important practices that a manager can employ to help drive a successful outcome from a project. Good risk management allows organizations to proactively respond to risks.

Unfortunately, many managers believe risk management to be too time consuming or too complicated. Some find it to be shrouded in mystery.

This book by Dr. John J. Byrne, PMP is designed to demystify risk management, explaining introductory and advanced risk management approaches in simple language. This book uses real-life examples from a very influential project that helped change the course of world history -- the project that designed and built the *Polaris* missile and accompanying submarine launch system that became a key deterrent to a Soviet nuclear attack during the Cold War.

Containing a foreword by James R. Snyder, one of the founders of the Project Management Institute (PMI), this book is structured to align with the risk management approach described in PMI's the *Project Management Body of Knowledge (PMBOK Guide)*.

ISBN-13:   9781554890972 (Paperback)

Available in print and electronic formats. Order from your local bookseller, Amazon.com, or directly from the publisher at **www.mmpubs.com**.

Agile Leadership and the Management of Change: Project Lessons from Winston Churchill and the Battle of Britain

Around the turn of the millennium, there was a poll conducted in Britain that asked who people thought was the most influential person in all of Britain's history. The winner: Winston Churchill. What set Churchill above the others was his leadership qualities: his ability to create and share a powerful vision, his ability to motivate the population in the face of tremendous fear, and his ability to get others to rally behind him and quickly turn his visions into reality. By any measure, Winston Churchill was a powerful leader.

What many don't know, however, was how Churchill used his leadership skills to restructure the British military, government, and even the British manufacturing sector to support his efforts to rearm the country and get ready for an imminent enemy invasion in early 1940.

Join author Mark Kozak-Holland as he explores how Churchill acted as the head project manager of a massive change project that affected the daily lives of millions of people. Learn about Churchill's change management and agile management techniques and how they can be applied to today's projects.

ISBN-13:   9781554890354   (Paperback)

Available in print and electronic formats. Order from your local bookseller, Amazon.com, or directly from the publisher at
www.mmpubs.com.

www.ingramcontent.com/pod-product-compliance
Lightning Source LLC
Chambersburg PA
CBHW071839230426
43671CB00012B/2011